Hug Someone You
Love Today

Hug Someone You Love Today

And How to Leave Your Personal Signature

Michael A. Pickles

Order this book online at www.trafford.com
or email orders@trafford.com

Most Trafford titles are also available at major online book retailers.

Printed in the United States of America.

ISBN: 978-1-4269-9622-1 (sc)
ISBN: 978-1-4269-9621-4 (hc)
ISBN: 978-1-4269-9620-7 (e)

Library of Congress Control Number: 2011963564

Trafford rev. 02/07/2012

 www.trafford.com

North America & international
toll-free: 1 888 232 4444 (USA & Canada)
phone: 250 383 6864 ♦ fax: 812 355 4082

Contents

Forward...ix

Acknowledgments.. xiii

About the Author xv

The Hug!...1

Electric Company...2

Trimming the Excess Fat 3

A Father's Final Wishes..4

The Surrogate Mother..6

Hugs along the Appalachian Trail 8

A Train Ride to Happiness 9

Slow but Steady Wins the Race...11

A Hug Can Save a Life 12

What I Learned From a Dog...13

Hugs of Humanity...14

Huggies at Summer Camp 18

Flying High in the Clouds..19

Necessary Life Struggles..20

You Light Up My Life...22

Love in a Cup 23

Earning a Child's Trust 25

Keep It Simple Stupid...26

Only a Phone Call Away..27

An Elephant is an Elephant or is it? 28

Random Hugs of Kindness 29

Teenage Huggers..30

If at First You Don't Succeed, Try, Try Again....................31

The Bigger, the Better 32

The Art of Hugging..33

Philosophically Speaking...34

A Loss for Words 35

Don't Ever...37

Over 100 People Served..39

Child's Meaning of Love 40

Free Hugs Campaigns from Around the World...................42

The True Value of Time...43

Pay it forward..46

Ice-cream Kindness...47

Hugged by an Angel..48

I've Learned That..49

Cowboy Mouths 54

Those beside You...55

Wearing your "Stuff" on your Sleeve...................................56

DO IT ANYWAY 58

Life's Major League Curveballs 60

Bucket List to Freedom..61

An Unforgettable Gift 62

Always Remain Curious 63

The Starfish 64

The Wizardly Power of Belief 65

A Picture is worth a Thousand Words..................................66

Surfing to Higher Heights 68

Changing the World One Hamburger at a Time..................69

Wings of Protection 70

From Punching Bag to World Champion 71

A Wife's Never Ending Love 73

The Trouble Tree 75

Your Inner Butterfly 77

Is My Attitude Worth Catching? 78

Theory of a Thousand Marbles 79

No Laughing Matter..80

Pulling Together as a Team 81

Food for Thought 82

Turn Up Your Inner Heat 83

The Top Five Percent 84

Keep Your Chin Up...85

Living Life through a TV Screen..................................86

Brotherly Love...87

Call it Puppy Love 88

The Power of Visualization 90

Don't Quit...91

Enough for a Tip...93

De-stressing from a Child's Love.................................94

I Love You, I Forgive You and Good Night Mother....95

Rocks and Sand.. 102

Bad Company 104

Money Matters... 105

What Goes Around Comes Around 106

Your Life's Legacy 108

Secret to Living a Long Life..................................... 109

Footprints 110

Find Your "Delete All" Button 111

An Honorable 67 Minutes.. 112

Changing the World One Pencil at a Time 114

How Much Is Time Worth?...................................... 119

Final Curtain Call.. 120

Forward

I WOULD LIKE to share with you a personal story, a story that touched me deeply and demonstrates the fundamental message behind this book. As you will clearly see, the events of this story planted the seeds for this book.

During my fourth year of teaching, I had the great privilege of working with an amazing lady, an educator by the name of Miss Bezanson. She taught a grade four class to whom I taught Physical Education. Therefore, I had the opportunity to communicate with her on a daily basis.

About six months into the school year, Miss Bezanson gave me something that would forever change my teaching techniques and my life, although I did not realize it at that moment.

One afternoon, I was in Miss Bezanson's class discussing a student who was displaying increasing behavioural problems in my Physical Education class. Sensing I was experiencing tremendous stress as a result of this student, she gave me something that touched my heart and reinforced an important life lesson. She handed me a small paper card entitled "Hug Someone You Love Today".

That was it! No preachy sermon or fancy teaching strategies. At that moment, I realized that maybe all that child needed was a simple hug, a sign of affection, which he may or may not have been receiving at home. So the next day, I gave him a "Hug Someone You Love Today" card. From that day forward, I never had another major problem with that student. I will never forget that experience. It was absolutely amazing, a small miracle!

More recently I read a story by Barbara Glanz, who suggested that every one of us should endeavor to make a difference in the world and create some sort of *personal signature* that will not only encourage and motivate ourselves, but others as well.

For example, she pointed out a baggage attendant who collected all the luggage tags that fell off of customer's suitcases. Usually these tags are thrown into the garbage. Not this attendant. In his free time, he would send the tags back to their rightful owners with a note saying "Thank you for flying with us". That was his personal signature.

I decided that my personal signature would come from my life changing experience with Miss Bezanson so many years ago. I would collect hug stories from people; stories about normal folks like you and I, whose lives have been positively changed as a result of receiving or given a simple hug. As a result, my book *"Hug Someone You Love Today: and How to Leave Your Personal Signature"* was written.

The purpose of this book is to inspire you to be happy, to live a life filled with purpose and to take action. As you read these touching stories, hopefully you will begin to feel more peaceful and more loving yourself. Life doesn't just happen to you, you make it happen. So re-read *"Hug Someone You Love Today: and How to Leave Your Personal Signature"* as many times as necessary to stay enriched, motivated and inspired. This book is my personal signature to you. Together we can *change the world one hug at a time.*

Acknowledgments

THIS AMAZING BOOK has been a personal journey for me and has taken many years to write. To say this book was solely written by Mike Pickles is far from the truth. No book can be written without the contribution and assistance of others. So many people have helped me with this book, or influenced some of the ideas that are found in it, that this book would surely not have been written without you. So thank you to everyone for your generous contributions.

First and foremost, I want to thank and acknowledge everyone who submitted their hug stories, without which this book would never have been written. You are truly the essence of this book. Thank you all so very much!

A heartfelt thank you goes out to my editing/publishing team Trafford Publishing, who put up with all the endless corrections, revisions and deadlines. Also, a special thank you to my check-in coordinator Nika Corales, who kept me motivated and on track. Thank you all so very much!

I may have forgotten to mention others, who have helped me with the writing, editing and publishing of this book, so please accept my apologies and know that you are all greatly remembered and appreciated.

I would also like to express a sincere thanks to all our families; parents, siblings, partners and children, whose support, past, present and future, makes it all worthwhile.

Finally, a special thank you goes out to my amazing son Sebastian who keeps me dreaming, and to my always supportive life friend Robyn, who keeps me grounded. I love you both dearly!

About the Author

MICHAEL A. PICKLES was born in Digby, Nova Scotia, Canada. He has been teaching for seventeen years within Canada. He has also taught overseas; once in Malawi, Africa and twice in Guyana and Ecuador, South America.

Michael has been published in many newspaper articles, and was co-authored in a book entitled "*The Path to Success*" alongside The Secret guru Sandy Forster. He is currently teaching the Nunavut Teacher Education Program (NTEP) for the Nunavut Arctic College in Rankin Inlet, Nunavut, Canada with his amazing son.

The Hug!

It's wonderous what a hug can do.

A hug can cheer you when you're blue.

A hug can say, "I love you so,"

Or, "Gee, I hate to see you go."

A hug is, "Welcome back again."

And "Great to see you! Where've you been?"

A hug can soothe a small child's pain,

and bring a rainbow after rain.

The hug! There's just no doubt about it—

we scarcely could survive without it!

A hug delights and warms and charms.

It must be why God gave us arms.

A hug can break the language barrier,

and make your travels so much merrier.

No need to fret about your store of 'em,

the more you give, the more there's more of 'em.

So stretch those arms without delay

and give someone a hug today!

-Author Unknown

"Sometimes you have to fall from the mountain to realize what you are climbing for."

—*Chae Richardosn*

Electric Company

When I first met my boyfriend, it was love at the first sight. After a few weeks, we held hands for the very first time. The second we touched I felt an electric shock, and he felt it too. It was such a strong and powerful feeling that we both got scared and immediately let go of each other's hand.

A few days later we hugged for the very first time. That hug was the craziest hug ever! The electricity we felt was so strong that we didn't want to let go of each other. Since that day, every hug has been the same . . . powerful. Even after five years together, they are still the best hugs in my life!

Isa Clonada
Quito, Ecuador

> *"You don't get in life what you want. You get what you are."*
> —*Les Brown*

Trimming the Excess Fat

If you have ever participated in a Triathlon, and I haven't, you would know that it's not an easy task. Even more difficult would be to win it six times, as is the case with Dave Scott.

It was reported that for his training, Dave Scott would ride his bike 175 miles, swim 20,000 meters, than run 17 miles every single day. Furthermore, a man who easily burned 5,000 calories a day relied on a low fat, high carbohydrate diet.

Trimming himself of that excess fat was one more step that he believed would make him that much better, would get him to the finish line that much quicker, and it gave him that extra edge over all the other athletes. His discipline paid off, since he won the Hawaii Ironman Triathlon an amazing six times.

Everyone would like to be the best, but most lack the discipline to turn their potential into reality. It all lies in the discipline to do whatever it takes to become the best within your selected field and then to seek continual improvement. It's really that simple.

"Even if you are on the right track, you'll get run over if you just sit there."
—Will Rogers

A Father's Final Wishes

January 11, 2005 was the day my life drastically changed. I received news that my Dad had cancer. It was an aggressive cancer and it was terminal. The doctors explained that his cancer started in his lungs and now had spread to several of his other organs.

Dad had been warned many times before to quit smoking, he even had an angioplasty done to his legs due to poor circulation problems related to smoking. On top of it all, he was a fireman who smoked a pack and a half a day. I was always telling him to quit smoking, you're too young to smoke and you have bronchitis. Dad didn't listen and kept on smoking.

The doctors explained his x-rays. Dad's lungs were black from years of inhaling smoke from the many fires he was in and from his heavy smoking. He was becoming very sick and starting to lose his faculties. I went to visit him the next day and we talked for hours. It was awkward knowing that he didn't have much time left. That he'd be leaving me soon.

Dad then looked at me and said, "Do you want to end up like me? Please Denise, stop smoking before it kills you. You have health problems now from smoking. Promise me that you will quit smoking." I promised him that I would quit smoking. We then embarrassed in a big hug with tears in both of our eyes.

His words inspired me to quit smoking. I now have no breathing problems or bronchitis. I have been cigarette free for 15 years. My Dad lost his battle with cancer on February 21, 1995 at the age of 60. That's when my life truly began.

Denise Muise
Nova Scotia, Canada

"Enjoy the little things, for one day you may look back and realize they were the big things."

—*Robert Brault*

The Surrogate Mother

A police officer opens up a shed door to find a griping dog. It was dirty, malnourished, and had clearly been abused. In an act of kindness, the officer took the greyhound female dog to the nearby Wildlife Sanctuary known as a haven for animals abandoned, orphaned or otherwise in need.

The sanctuary staff immediately went to work with two goals: to restore the dog to full health, and to win her trust. It took several weeks, but eventually both goals were achieved. They named her Jasmine, and they started to think about finding her an adoptive home.

No-one remembers how it began, but Jasmine started welcoming all animal arrivals at the sanctuary. It wouldn't matter if it was a puppy, a fox cub, or a rabbit, Jasmine would peer into their cage and deliver a welcoming lick.

One of the workers remembers. "We had two puppies that had been abandoned by a nearby railway line. One was a Lakeland Terrier cross and another was a Jack Russell Doberman cross. Jasmine approached them and grabbed one by the scruff of the neck in her mouth and put him on the sofa. Then she fetched the other one and sat down with them, cuddling them."

"But she is like that with all of our animals, even the rabbits. She takes all the stress out of them and it helps them to not only feel close to her but to settle into their new surroundings. She has done the same with the fox and badger cubs; she licks the rabbits and guinea pigs and even lets the birds perch on the bridge of her nose."

Jasmine, the abused and deserted dog became the animal sanctuary's surrogate mother. Even animals clearly know the power of affection and given hugs. Jasmine was simply doing what she does best . . . being a mother.

"Love understands all languages."

—*Romanian Proverb*

Hugs along the Appalachian Trail

You may not be aware of this, but there was a guy who hiked the entire 2,200 mile Appalachian Trail a few years back who called himself "Free Hugs". He pretty much hugged everyone he met along the way. I thought this might be of interest. It's certainly something to thin about.

Steve Silberberg

"Do not go where the path may lead; go instead where there is no path and leave a trial."

—*Ralph Waldo Emerson*

A Train Ride to Happiness

In April of 1987, I hopped on a train in East Africa bound for Dar es Salaam, the capital of Tanzania. I had been given a sleeping cabin with two other women and their three small children. It was hot, humid, and overcrowded, but the price was right.

It had only been a few days since I said goodbye to Wayne, my lover and traveling companion. Wayne was a New Zealander and I was a Canadian whose travelling itineraries crossed paths in Turkey. We became inseparable for the next eight months traveling throughout Europe, and with plans to explore Africa together.

In Nairobi, Wayne was hospitalized for malaria. The illness and condition of the hospital was daunting for him, and he wanted to leave Africa early. To this day, I don't know why I said; "no" when he asked me to accompany him back to New Zealand. Perhaps it was the fear of commitment or a belief that I didn't deserve his love, either way, I found myself travelling solo again.

Not long into the ride, the train unexpectedly slowed down and came to a complete stop. I would have asked my cabin mates if they knew what was going on, but my knowledge of the Swahili language was very limited.

We soon realized that something was wrong. Slowly dozens of passengers wondered off the train into the hot, dry desert. Exhausted and feeling nauseous, I only made it as far as the landing steps and slumped down on the top stair.

As I stared out into the empty abyss, my whole being was suddenly consumed with an overwhelming feeling of regret, sadness, and emptiness. I realized right then that I had never felt such a high degree of loneliness combined with self-pity in my life. I was paralyzed with grief and a longing to be back with Wayne.

Then a miracle happened. Two young African children approached me. Their dark, curious eyes gazed at my pale skin and their little hands reached out to touch my bare arms. They stroked my skin with such care and gentleness that I responded with a hug.

As I held these desert angels, I felt my spirit restored. Joy and relief filled my being and I didn't feel alone anymore.

Trudi D'Ambrumenil
BC, Canada

"The only journey is the journey within."

—Rainer Maria Rilke

Slow but Steady Wins the Race

The story of Sam Walton reminds me of the famous quote from the Chinese philosopher Lao-tzu. "A journey of a thousand miles must begin with a single step."

Sam Walton, a humble businessman from Arkansas, began building his dream in 1945 with a single dime store. He didn't open his second store until years later. Walton slowly built his business step by step until a quarter of a century later he had accumulated a chain of 38 Wal-Marts.

According to the Forbes Global 2000 list, Wal-Mart is the biggest private employer in the world with over 2 million employees, and is the largest and most successful retail store chain in history. In order to be successful, Sam Walton clearly changed what needed to be changed and not what was easy to change, and that made all the difference.

"Procrastination is attitude's natural assassin. There's nothing as fatiguing as an uncompleted task."

—Psychologist William James

A Hug Can Save a Life

Twin girls, Brielle and Kyrie, were born 12 weeks ahead of their due date. Needing intensive care, they were placed in separate incubators.

Kyrie began to gain weight and her health stabilized. But Brielle, born only 2 lbs, had trouble breathing, heart problems and other complications. She was not expected to live.

Their nurse did everything she could to make Brielle's health better, but nothing she did was helping. With nothing else to do, their nurse went against hospital policy and decided to place both babies in the same incubator.

She left the twin girls to sleep and when she returned she found a sight she could not believe. She called all the nurses and doctors and this is what they saw.

As Brielle got closer to her sister, Kyrie put her small little arm around her, as if to hug and support her sister. From that moment on, Brielle's breathing and heart rate stabilized and her health became normal. From then on, they decided to keep both babies together, because when they were together they kept each other alive.

Dr. Jeff Mullan

"There is no strength without unity."

—Irish Proverb"

What I Learned From a Dog

1. Never pass up an opportunity to go for a joy ride.
2. Allow the experience of fresh air and the wind in your face.
3. When loved ones come home, always run to greet them.
4. When it's in your best interest, always practice obedience.
5. Let others know when they've invaded your territory.
6. Take naps and always stretch before rising.
7. Run, romp, and play daily.
8. Eat with gusto and enthusiasm.
9. Be loyal.
10. Never pretend to be something you're not.
11. If what you want lies buried, dig until you find it.
12. When someone is having a bad day, be silent, sit close by and nuzzle them gently.
13. Delight in the simple joy of a long walk.
14. Avoid biting when a simple growl will do.
15. When you are happy, dance around and wag your entire body.

"A friend is one who knows us, but loves us anyway."

—*Jerome Cummings*

Hugs of Humanity

It is late Sunday morning and I am glancing around my classroom—maps, posters, student art works, professional art works by former students, odd collections of photographs from magazines and of students engaged in learning, teaching tools, plants, tables and desks. My life! I am incapable of separating my personal self from my teacher self because the two are intermingled in my love of Art and Social Studies, and from the core of my values and beliefs—beginning with the 4 h's—honour, humour, humility, and honesty; followed by 3c's—curiosity, courage and creative problem solving; 2 s's self-discipline and spirituality; and ending with Balance. I capitalize the word "balance" because, for all of us, each day is a high wire act where balance is critical to survival and development as a human being. I also believe that within this balance lays our greatest potential for humanity.

The profession of teaching found me later in life, and it did not take long to realize that it is an extremely difficult and complex vocation. In my 19th year as a teacher, I entered the darkest period of my career and in that personal hell I also received two hugs of humanity.

My darkest period began with three students. It was a week before Christmas Break and I was making my way through the school to the Guidance Department when I encountered three boys relaxing at a table in our cafeteria. It did not take long to find out they were skipping their classes. My copious pleads of "get to class" were ignored with silence and smirks. As one of them slowly started to get up and do the right thing, I took a deep breath of relief, turned and walked away.

I stopped dead in my tracks after one of the three boys directed a rude remark towards me. I turned and waited until he walked into my personal space. "Would you care to explain that to Administration?" I asked breathing shallowly and with a dead-pan face for fear of losing my temper. His response was a hard punch on the upper part of my right arm. "Smack!" The light inside of me went out.

I was shocked. Even now, years later, all I can recall are their laughter and mocking looks on their turned faces as they ran down the hallway. Never had I been physically assaulted by a student! And I certainly never saw this one coming! I just stood there gazing down that hallway until they turned the corner.

What followed is the typical bureaucratic shuffle—identifying the students (I only knew one of them); talking with administration; writing up my report; administration holding meetings with the students in question and their parents. For the most part, I was not involved, but rather expected to continue as if nothing had happened.

Whenever I had a rare moment alone, I just sat and gazed into space . . . no thoughts . . . no feelings . . . just gazing. Night time was even worse as I could hardly sleep and when I did, horrific nightmares woke me. My life had been instantly transformed from being purposeful to nothingness. It was in this personal dark hell that I gradually received two important, unexpected and unconventional hugs.

As a general rule, I remain each day in my classroom until about 5pm. After the attack, I decided that I needed to break this rule and head home as soon as possible in an effort to look after myself. This would never happen.

On my first day of resolve to 'look after myself', Tai Mary Mikkigak arrived in my classroom to ask if I could help her create a painting as a Christmas gift for her mother. Enthusiastically, she went on to explain that she found a black and white archival photograph of her grandmother on the Internet. The picture had been taken in the 1970's in the hamlet of Cape Dorset, on Baffin Island, in the territory that is known today as Nunavut. For quite some time, I examined the kind, sweet face of Tai's grandmother. There was something about her face that spoke to me of hardship that I more than likely will never know in my lifetime. In so many ways, she reminded me of my mother, grandmother and great grandmother—all strong courageous women who led harder lives than I. "Of course I will work with you to make this painting." I responded smilingly at Tai.

For the next five days, Tai and I worked after school until we created her mother's Christmas gift. The process of working alongside Tai to capture her grandmother's essence and her life in Cape Dorset in paint eventually became a very loud message for me. "You are a teacher because you are passionate about your subjects and your students' learning. It is your purpose in this life." Without knowing it, Tai Mikkigak had given me a heartfelt hug that catapulted my inevitable healing.

On the first day back from Christmas Break, I received a hand-written thank you note from Tai's mother—Moatie Mikkigak—expressing how much she appreciated the painting. She ended her note by stating, "Thank you for being such a good art teacher." Tears swelled into my eyes when I read this. The physical assault had left me feeling anything but a 'good teacher'. Yet Moatie Mikkigak clearly thought otherwise.

My wise godmother had told me repeatedly that life lessons and helping spirits are like pearls strung together. Within a lifetime, each person creates his/her own string of pearls. On my necklace, the pearls known as Tai and Moatie are two of the biggest and shiniest.

"Thank you Tai Mary Mikkigak and Moatie Mikkigak for giving me the most uplifting hugs of my teaching career to date! In doing so, you have shown me true humanity."

Betty L. E. Wilcox
Northwest Territories, Canada

"My goal for myself is to reach the highest level of humanity that is possible for me."

—Oprah Winfrey

Huggies at Summer Camp

I remember when I was younger and I was at a Girl Guide Camp that we had a different theme everyday. One day happened to be 'Hug Day'. Since I was such a social child, I hugged every camper/leader when they were near me. So by the end of the day my nickname was Huggies, not to be confused with the diaper brand.

Kelsie Trenholm
Nova Scotia, Canada

"May you live all the days of your life."
—*Jonathan Swift*

Flying High in the Clouds

Until the 1950's, Boeing focused on building aircraft for the military, specifically designing bombers. Boeing had no existence in the commercial aircraft industry. Today, nearly all air travel takes place on a Boeing jet. How did this accomplishment happen?

Throughout the 1940's, Boeing intentionally stayed away from the commercial aircraft industry which was teeming by smaller, propeller-driven planes. But in 1950, relying on their knowledge of building jets for the military, Boeing eagerly jumped on the opportunity to enter into the commercial aircraft arena by building bigger aircraft with jet engines.

Three decades later, Boeing was known as one of the best commercial aircraft builders in the world, and had built five of the most thriving commercial jets in aviation history; the Boeing 707, 727, 737, 747, and the Boeing 757. To get what you've never had, you must do what you've never done. What a great example of following one's passion, taking a risk and flying high in the clouds to reach one's dreams.

"It takes less work to succeed than fail."

—*W. Clement Stone*

Necessary Life Struggles

A man found a cocoon of a moth. He took it home so that he could watch the moth come out of the cocoon. On the day a small opening appeared, he sat and watched the moth for several hours as the moth struggled to force the body through that little hole. The moth seemed to be stuck and appeared to have stopped making progress. It seemed as if it had gotten as far as it could and it could go no farther.

The man, in his kindness, decided to help the moth; so he took a pair of scissors and snipped off the remaining bit of the cocoon. The moth then emerged easily. But its body was swollen and small, its wings wrinkled and shriveled. The man continued to watch the moth because he expected that, at any moment, the wings would enlarge and expand to and able to support the body, which would contract in time. Neither happened! It never was able to fly.

The man in his kindness did not understand that the struggle required for the moth to get through the tiny opening was necessary to force fluid from the body of the moth into its wings so that it would be ready for flight upon achieving its freedom from the cocoon. Freedom and flight would only come after the struggle. By depriving the moth of a struggle, he deprived the moth of live.

Sometimes struggles are exactly what we need in our life. If we were to go through our life without any obstacles, we would not be as strong as what we could have been. Give every opportunity a chance and don't forget the power in the struggle.

"One isn't necessarily born with courage, but one is born with potential. Without courage, we cannot practice any other virtue with consistency. We can't be kind, true, merciful, generous, or honest."

—*Maya Angelou*

You Light Up My Life

When my friend Scott Richards was dying of cancer, he told me that watching the original "Free Hugs" video made in Australia made him smile when he was getting down upon himself while lying around in his sterile hospital environment.

At around that period, I was shooting a film with a film crew I had hired for my executive coaching business. After we finished our days shoot, I asked them if they would head to downtown Minneapolis with me to make a "Free Hugs Minneapolis" video for my friend Scott. We did and it totally lit him up.

Scott has since past, and the video stands as a legacy to him. When I watch it I am reminded of the importance of compassion and friendship in my life.

Gary Cohen
Wayzata, Minneapolis

"Only when we give joyfully, without hesitation or thought of gain, can we truly know what love means.

—*Leo Buscaglia*

Love in a Cup

A group of alumni, highly established in their careers, got together to visit their old university professor. Conversation soon turned into complaints about stress in work and life.

Offering his guests coffee, the professor went to the kitchen and returned with a large pot of coffee and a range of cups—porcelain, plastic, glass, crystal, some plain looking, some expensive, some exquisite—telling them to help themselves to the coffee.

When all the students had a cup of coffee in hand, the professor said: "If you noticed, all the nice looking expensive cups were taken up, leaving behind the plain and cheap ones. While it is normal for you to want only the best for yourselves, that is the source of your problems and stress.

Be assured that the cup itself adds no quality to the coffee. In most cases it is just more expensive and in some cases even hides what we drink. What all of you really wanted was coffee, not the cup, but you consciously went for the best cups.

Now consider this: Life is the coffee; the jobs, money and position in society are the cups. They are just tools to hold and contain Life, and the type of cup we have does not define, nor change the quality of Life we live.

Sometimes, by concentrating only on the cup, we fail to enjoy the coffee God has provided us." God brews the coffee, not the cups—Enjoy your coffee!

"Let a joy keep you. Reach out your hands and take it when it runs by."
                                        —*Carl Sandburg*

Earning a Child's Trust

There is nothing like the hug a child. Whether receiving one or giving one, I can't narrow down my hug story to just one. As a Child and Youth Worker, the most important thing is gaining the trust of a child. Being the one they can trust, the one that won't judge them or harm them.

Sometimes that trust is earned within a month and other times, it could take several months to a year to accomplish. So when that moment of trust arrives, it is the ultimate reward.

So for me, when that child hugs me, I know that they trust me and they feel safe. For me it's not just one hug that has changed my life, it's several. To feel those little arms wrapped around you because you have made them realize that they are worth it, that they can succeed despite what life has thrown at them.

Whether it is helping a child gain social skills, helping a teen through some emotional distress or getting them into counseling, a hug is worth it all. After 20 years, each time I get a hug or a child lets me hug them, my day brightens right up and my heart fills with warmth. My job has once again fulfilled its purpose, bettering the life of a child!

Michelle Cairns
Ontario, Canada

"The purpose of life is to matter, to be productive, to have it make some difference that you lived at all."

—Leo Rosten

Keep It Simple Stupid

Is your life simple or complex? I'm reminded of an ancient Greek parable, "The Fox and Hedgehog" when I ponder about the simplicity of life.

The fox is very cunning, fast, and sleek, and is able to formulate many complex strategies for sneak attacks upon the hedgehog. In comparison, the hedgehog is slow, waddles, and spends most of his day searching for food.

Every day, the fox circles around the hedgehog's den waiting for the perfect opportunity to leap upon the hedgehog in sudden victory. Due to his fast, sleek stature, the fox surely looks like the winner.

One day, the hedgehog wanders right into the unsuspecting path of the fox. The fox leaps out in front of the hedgehog with lightning speed saying, "I've got you now!" The hedgehog sensing danger immediately rolls into a perfect ball of spikes. The fox sees his defense and reluctantly pulls back his attack and walks away.

Each day, some similar version of this battle between the fox and the hedgehog continues. Despite the craftiness nature of the fox, the hedgehog always wins. Is it due to luck or chance? No, the hedgehog reduces all challenges to simple ideas or principles. They understand that the core of profound insight is simplicity. As my father would often say, "Keep it simple stupid." (aka KISS)

"Most men would rather die, than think. Many do."
—*Bertrand Russell*

Only a Phone Call Away

I recently moved to Miami, Florida to do my Master's Degree in Psychology. Coming from Ecuador, moving away to better my education but leaving my family behind brought lots of mixed emotions for me.

One day I was really feeling sad and lonely, you could even say I was in a depressed mood. The only close person I have here in Miami is my cousin Juan. Feeling my anxiety escalating further, I texted him to come over.

While I waited, I tried to distract myself doing homework and some meaningless chores, but nothing would rid me of my despair. All of a sudden Juan walked into my door and gave me the warmest hug I've ever felt in my life. All of my tension, anxiety, and sadness vanished within seconds of that one special hug. It was amazing!

He didn't have to speak a single word to comfort me, it was his strong loving hug that brought me back to earth and made me feel peaceful inside. Now I truly understand how strong and powerful our body energies are and why we should all offer hugs more often.

Pamela Proano
Quito, Ecuador

"A person who talks all the time knows nothing. A person who truly knows things, talks very little."

—*Lao Tzu*

An Elephant is an Elephant or is it?

According to the Oxford Dictionary, perception is the ability to see, hear or become aware of something through our senses. There is a famous Indian story, "The Blind Men and the Elephant," which clearly elaborates this brief definition.

A king summoned four blind men who had no idea of what an elephant looked like. The king asked them to stand in a circle around the elephant, each touching a different part of the elephant. Then the king said, "This is an elephant. Now you each tell me what an elephant is."

The blind man who touched the side of the elephant said that an elephant was like a giant wall. The blind man who touched the trunk terrifyingly said it was like a long snake. The blind man who examined the tail said it was like a rope. The last blind man who was touching the leg said, "My king, an elephant is like a tree trunk."

Our thoughts about things that surround us are greatly influenced by our perception. That perception is limited. The past exists as a reminder or a fading memory. The present immediately becomes the past as soon as we perceive it, and we do not know the future; it exists only in our imaginations. Always keep your perception open.

"There are things known and there are things unknown, and in between are the doors of perception."

—*Aldous Huxley*

Random Hugs of Kindness

I come from a very huggy family. Years ago, I was at the check-out line at the local grocery store and the woman behind me was fumbling with her items. I helped her put some things on the conveyor belt and she thanked me and then apologized. She said, "I guess I'm not myself today. My mother died." I told her there was no need to apologize and I replied, "I'm so sorry for your loss." And I hugged her. I felt her take a deep breath and relax into my arms. The whole thing didn't last very long, but I know that she left a little lighter.

More recently, I attended a Jerry Stocking seminar. He sent us on a scavenger hunt. There were a lot of things on the list (get on the radio or TV, buy a pair of shoes for under $5 & get a discount & find someone to give them to, get a free lunch somewhere, go to a senior citizen's center and sing a song, etc. all while staying in contact with a partner). On the list was also to give a hug to a man & a woman you didn't know.

We started off by checking our items off the list, but eventually we were just hugging everyone! The first was an undertaker at a funeral home. Everyone was very receptive and we left a lot of smiles along the way—waitresses, check-out clerks, and other shoppers in the stores. We hugged them all!

Hali Chambers
Virginia, USA

"Life's not about waiting for the storms to pass; it's about learning to dance in the rain."

—*Vivian Greene*

Teenage Huggers

On Thanksgiving weekend, I went to see the movie "Australia" (where I used to live) with my aunt, who's a 70-something nun (no habit). When we came out of the movie theater, which is in an upscale open-air mall in Palm Beach Gardens, FL, there were three teenagers outside. One was holding a sign that said, "Would you like a hug?" The two teenage girls said hello to us as we passed by and asked if we'd like a hug. We both laughed and hugged them and said thank you, then went on our way, laughing at the gesture, but also feeling pretty good about ourselves. I don't know if they had any other takers, but I'm glad we hugged them.

Ellen Cannon
Florida, USA

> *"Life is not worth living unless it is lived for others."*
> —*Mother Teresa*

If at First You Don't Succeed, Try, Try Again

One day I took lunch at a small mall about a ten minute walk away from my office. I had the idea of given out hugs, but I wanted it to be totally spontaneous, so I only targeted folks who were close enough to hug. The first two were a young lady and then a little boy about five years old, who ran away from me. The third, a teenaged girl, smiled and then ran to get some friends. They watched my every move after that.

I guess it doesn't make sense to them. The next time I decide to give out hugs in the mall, I'll have to watch out for Security. In the meantime, it definitely gave a whole group of people something to talk about over their lunch hour and probably that evening at their dinner tables as well.

Gary Dale
Bangkok, Thailand

"It does not matter how slowly you go so long as you do not stop."
—Confucius

The Bigger, the Better

I am a recovered compulsive overeater. When I have the opportunity to hug another compulsive overeater-stranger, it is more fulfilling than hugging a non-compulsive overeater-stranger. The more obese a person, the more fulfilling *giving* the hug is to me.

I think the reason that hugging a larger person is more fulfilling than a smaller one for me is because I know that as a compulsive overeater (with a daily reprieve), that the only way I have been given this freedom, the weight loss and maintain it daily, is through working with other hopeless compulsive overeaters.

The way that I was set free from my food addiction was through being loved by someone who was recovering themselves. Now, giving to another compulsive overeater feeds my soul—the more hopeless, the more pleasure I get from giving that hug.

Dr. Talia Witkowski

"The most powerful and predictable people-builders are praise and encouragement."

—*Brain Tracy*

The Art of Hugging

I hug strangers on a weekly basis and I teach people how to hug well. The comments I get on my hugs are that they feel transformative and safe. I have had strangers cry in my arms as I softly held them and breathed with them. I have been thanked for being a safe place to feel loved.

Hugging is an art form whether with kids, friends, strangers or our loved ones. The art to hugging is being lost today in the fears of sexual harassment, teachers worrying about policies and strangers worrying about misinterpreted intent.

I teach that hugs should be full body, (not tenting) and should incorporate harmonious breathing and a relaxing feel with each other. They should be longer than 30 seconds and should not include ending with "patting" or "thumping". Gently gliding in and out with eye contact before and after makes a hug a gesture of healing and is very profound for many people.

Tanja Diamond

"I love hugging. I wish I was an octopus, so I could hug ten people at a time."

—*Drew Barrymore*

Philosophically Speaking

Here's a quiz.

1. Name the last five Heisman trophy winners.
2. Name five people who have won the Pulitzer Prize.
3. Name the last half dozen Academy Award winners for best actor and actress.

How did you do? Yes they are the best in their fields. But the ovation dies, awards tarnish, and achievements are forgotten.

Here's another quiz.

1. List a few teachers who aided your journey through school.
2. Name three friends who have helped you through a difficult time.
5. Think of five people you enjoy spending time with.

Easier? I bet it was much easier to answer. The people who make a difference in your life are not the ones with the most credentials, the most money, or the most awards. They are the ones that care.

> *"No act of kindness, no matter how small is ever wasted."*
>
> —*Aesop*

A Loss for Words

As a Funeral Celebrant, I hug strangers all the time at memorial services. One night, I conducted an annual memorial and a candle lighting service at a funeral home. I received many hugs from strangers after the service. One 16 year old girl approached me in tears saying briefly that her father recently died. I gave her a hug. That single hug led her to share her story, which was not easy for such a young girl.

She said that she listened to every word I said during the service. An idea came to her while I was speaking and she explained that she planned to include her father in the Christmas holiday by having everyone in her family write a memory on a piece of paper and hang the notes on the tree. She was so proud of her discovery that memories of her father could be included this year. At the end of our exchange, she was smiling through her tears. She just needed someone to care and listen. A single hug opened up the opportunity for her to share her vision for a new holiday without her dad.

Especially in dealing with death and funerals, I have found that a hug speaks loudly when we are at a loss for words. I often tell everyone "If you don't know what to say to the immediate family, a hug will say it for you." As a result of my encouragement to hug, at one service I conducted for a young baby, every single person in the church hugged the parents. I will never forget that service because everyone waited patiently in line to give them hugs. Every hug captured the depths of the pain and loss as we all shared tears. The word "sorry" just didn't seem like enough and so the hugs truly enveloped a moment that was so hard for everyone to express in words.

Pam Vetter

"For the believer, there is no question; for the nonbeliever, there is no answer."

—*Anonymous*

Don't Ever

Don't ever try to understand everything.
Some things will just never make sense.

Don't ever be reluctant to show your feelings.
When you're happy, give into it!
When you're not, live with it.

Don't ever be afraid to try to make things better.
You might be surprised at the results.

Don't ever take the weight of the world on your shoulders.

Don't ever feel threatened by the future.
Take life one day at a time.

Don't ever feel guilty about the past. What's done is done.
Learn from any mistakes you might have made.

Don't ever feel that you are alone.
There is always somebody there for you to reach out to.

Don't ever forget that you can achieve so many of the things
      you can imagine.
Imagine that! It's not as hard as it seems.

Don't ever stop loving.
Don't ever stop believing.

Don't ever stop dreaming your dreams.

—Author Unknown

"You're not obligated to win. You're obligated to keep trying to do the best you can every day."
—*Marian Wright Edelman*

Over 100 People Served

I regularly participate in "Free Hugs" events here in Austin where we hug at least 100 strangers in a couple of hours. Continue to promote the "Free Hugs" campaigns.

Taylor
Austin, Texas

"Understand that a man is worth just so much as the things are worth about which he busies himself."

—*Marcus Aurelius*

Child's Meaning of Love

A group of professionals posed this question to a group of 4 to 8 year-olds, "What does love mean?" The answers were deeper than anyone could have imagined.

"When my grandmother got arthritis, she couldn't bend over and paint her toenails anymore. So my grandfather does it for her all the time, even when his hands got arthritis too. That's love." Rebecca—age 8

When someone loves you, the way they say your name is different. You know that your name is safe in their mouth." Billy—age 4

"Love is when a girl puts on perfume and a boy puts on shaving cologne and they go out and smell each other." Karl—age 5

"Love is when you go out to eat and give somebody most of your French fries without making them give you any of theirs." Chrisy—age 6

"Love is what makes you smile when you're tired." Terri—age 4

Love is when my mommy makes coffee for my daddy and she takes a sip before giving it to him, to make sure the taste is OK." Danny—age 7

"Love is what's in the room with you at Christmas if you stop opening presents and listen," Bobby—age 7

"If you want to learn to love better, you should start with a friend who you hate," Nikka—age 6

"There are two kinds of love. Our love. God's love. But God makes both kinds of them." Jenny—age 8

"Love is when you tell a guy you like his shirt, then he wears it every day." Noelle—age 7

"Love is like a little old woman and a little old man who are still friends even after they know each other so well." Tommy—age 6

"My mommy loves me more than anybody. You don't see anyone else kissing me to sleep at night." Clare—age 6

"Love is when Mommy gives Daddy the best piece of chicken." Elaine—age 5

"Love is when Mommy sees Daddy smelly and sweaty and still says he is handsomer than Robert Redford." Chris—age 7

"I know my older sister loves me because she gives me all her old clothes and has to go out and buy new ones." Lauren—age 4

"Love is when Mommy sees Daddy on the toilet and she doesn't think it's gross." Mark—age 6

"To love deeply in one direction makes us more loving in all others."
—Anne-Sophie Swetchine

Free Hugs Campaigns from Around the World

Take a look at these . . . Free Hugs Campaigns from around the world. Maybe start a campaign in your area. Hey, it's free!

http://www.youtube.com/watch?v=1dPJphU6YOM&feature=related

http://www.youtube.com/watch?v=UF1mlQpqtws&feature=related

http://www.youtube.com/watch?v=XyA0eACdSng

http://www.youtube.com/watch?v=bH6QUgrD8DI&feature=related

Joe Palmer

*"They invented **hugs** to let people know you love them without saying anything."*

—*Bill Keane*

The True Value of Time

A young man learns what's most important in life from the guy next door. It had been some time since Jack had seen the old man. College, girls, career, and life itself got in the way. In fact, Jack moved clear across the country in pursuit of his dreams. There in the rush of his busy life, Jack had little time to think about the past and often no time to spend with his wife and son. He was working on his future, and nothing could stop him.

Over the phone, his mother told him, "Mr. Belser died last night. The funeral is Wednesday." Memories flashed through his mind like an old newsreel as he sat quietly remembering his childhood days.

"Jack, did you hear me?" "Oh, sorry Mom. Yes, I heard you. It's been so long since I thought of him. I'm sorry, but I honestly thought he died years ago," Jack said. "Well, he didn't forget you. Every time I saw him he'd ask how you were doing. He'd reminisce about the many days you spent over 'his side of the fence' as he put it."

"I loved that old house he lived in," Jack said. "You know, after your father died, Mr. Belser stepped in to make sure you had a man's influence in your life," she said. "He's the one who taught me carpentry," he said. "I wouldn't be in this business if it weren't for him. He spent a lot of time teaching me things he thought were important. Mom, I'll be there for the funeral," Jack said.

As busy as he was, he kept his word. Jack caught the next flight to his hometown. Mr. Belser's funeral was small and uneventful. He had no children of his own, and most of his relatives had passed away.

The night before he had to return home, Jack and his Mom stopped by to see the old house next door one more time. Standing in the doorway, Jack paused for a moment. It was like crossing over into another dimension, a leap through space and time. The house was exactly as he remembered. Every step held memories. Every picture, every piece of furniture . . . Jack stopped suddenly.

"What's wrong, Jack?" his Mom asked. "The box is gone," he said. "What box?" Mom asked. "There was a small gold box that he kept locked on top of his desk. I must have asked him a thousand times what was inside. All he'd ever tell me was 'the thing I value most,'" Jack said.

It was gone. Everything about the house was exactly how Jack remembered it, except for the box. He figured someone from the Belser family had taken it. "Now I'll never know what was so valuable to him," Jack said. "I better get some sleep. I have an early flight home, Mom."

It had been about two weeks since Mr. Belser died. Returning home from work one day Jack discovered a note in his mailbox. "Signature required on a package. No one at home. Please stop by the main post office within the next three days," the note read.

Early the next day Jack retrieved the package. The small box was old and looked like it had been mailed a hundred years ago. The handwriting was difficult to read, but the return address caught his attention. "Mr. Harold Belser" it read.

Jack took the box out to his car and ripped open the package. There inside was the gold box and an envelope. Jack's hands shook as he read the note inside. "Upon my death, please forward this box and its contents to Jack Bennett. It's the thing I valued most in my life." A small key was taped to the letter. His heart racing, as tears filling his eyes, Jack carefully unlocked the box. There inside he found a beautiful gold pocket watch. Running his fingers slowly over the finely etched casing, he unlatched the cover.

Inside he found these words engraved: "Jack, Thanks for your time! Harold Belser."

"The thing he valued most . . . was . . . my time."

Jack held the watch for a few minutes, then called his office and cleared his appointments for the next two days. "Why?" his assistant asked. "I need some time to spend with my son," he said.

—Author Unknown

"The bond that links your true family is not one of blood, but of respect and joy in each other's life."

—*Richard Bach*

Pay it forward

I enjoy given hugs. After the initial shock wears off, the most common response is along the lines of "Thanks, I really needed that." . . . to which I reply, "Pay it forward, I'm sure someone else could probably use one too."

Dr. Nicole K. Andrade
MA, USA

"We need 4 hugs a day for survival. We need 8 hugs a day for maintenance. We need 12 hugs a day for growth."

—*Virginia Satir*

Ice-cream Kindness

Last week I took my children to a restaurant. My six-year-old son asked if he could say grace. As we bowed our heads he said, "God is good. God is great. Thank you for the food, and I would even thank you more if Mom gets us ice cream for dessert. Amen!"

Along with the laughter from the other nearby customers, I heard a woman remark, "That's what's wrong with this country. Kids today don't even know how to pray. Asking God for ice-cream!"

Hearing this, my son burst into tears and asked me, "Did I do it wrong? Is God mad at me?" As I held him and assured him that he had done a terrific job and God was certainly not mad at him, an elderly gentleman approached the table. He winked at my son and said, "I happen to know that God thought that was a great prayer." "Really?" my son asked. "Cross my heart," the man replied.

Then in a whisper he added (indicating the woman whose remark had started this whole thing), "Too bad she never asks God for ice cream. A little ice cream is good for the soul sometimes." And then he walked away.

I bought my kids ice cream at the end of the meal. My son stared at his for a moment and then did something I will remember the rest of my life. He picked up his sundae and without a word, walked over and placed it in front of the woman. With a big smile he told her, "This is for you. Ice-cream is good for the soul sometimes; and my soul is good already."

"Everything has beauty, but not everyone sees it."

—*Confucius*

Hugged by an Angel

I was in a local hospital transporting a friend to an appointment. As I waited in the cafeteria with a cup of tea, I saw a tiny, grey haired woman with a big smile and bright eyes. She approached my table and asked if she could join me.

Linda was a former executive secretary, who had a job in the days when most women were not able to work outside the home. She'd battled breast cancer 10 years ago and now it was back with a vengeance.

Linda told me her story of challenge and triumph over illness, poverty, and faith. I was astounded by her positive attitude and knew she was giving me a gift by sharing her story.

When I hugged her goodbye, she said, "I'll see you in Heaven if I don't see you here again on this earth." I think I hugged an angel that day.

Lynne Klippel

"Millions of spiritual creatures walk the earth unseen, both when we wake and when we sleep."

—*John Milton*

I've Learned That

I've learned that you cannot make someone love you. All you can do is be someone who can be loved. The rest is up to them.

I've learned that no matter how much I care, some people just don't care back

I've learned that it takes years to build up trust, and only seconds to destroy it.

I've learned that it's not what you have in your life, but who you have in your life that counts.

I've learned that you shouldn't compare yourself to the best others can do, but to the best you can do.

I've learned that it's not what happens to people that's important. It's what they do about it.

I've learned that no matter how thin you slice it, there are always two sides.

I've learned that it's taking me a long time to become the person I want to be.

I've learned that it's a lot easier to react than it is to think.

I've learned that you should always leave loved ones with loving words. It may be the last time you see them.

I've learned that you can keep going long after you think you can't.

I've learned that we are responsible for what we do, no matter how we feel.

I've learned that either you control your attitude or it controls you.

I've learned that heroes are the people who do what has to be done when it needs to be done, regardless of the consequences.

I've learned that learning to forgive takes practice.

I've learned that there are people who love you dearly, but just don't know how to show it.

I've learned that money is a lousy way of keeping score.

I've learned that my best friend and I can do anything or nothing and have the best time.

I've learned that sometimes the people you expect to kick you when you're down will be the ones to help you get back up.

I've learned that I'm getting more and more like my grandma, and I'm kind of happy about it.

I've learned that sometimes when I'm angry I have the right to be angry, but that doesn't give me the right to be cruel.

I've learned that true friendship continues to grow, even over the longest distance. Same goes for true love.

I've learned that just because someone doesn't love you the way you want them to doesn't mean they don't love you with all they have.

I've learned that maturity has more to do with what types of experiences you've had and what you've learned from them and less to do with how many birthdays you've celebrated.

I've learned that you should never tell a child her dreams are unlikely or outlandish. Few things are more humiliating, and what a tragedy it would be if she believed it

I've learned that no matter how good a friend someone is, they're going to hurt you every once in a while and you must forgive them for that.

I've learned that it isn't always enough to be forgiven by others. Sometimes you have to learn to forgive yourself.

I've learned that no matter how bad your heart is broken the world doesn't stop for your grief.

I've learned that our background and circumstances may have influenced who we are, but we are responsible for who we become.

I've learned that sometimes when my friends fight, I'm forced to choose sides even when I don't want to.

I've learned that just because two people argue, it doesn't mean they don't love each other. And just because they don't argue, it doesn't mean they do.

I've learned that sometimes you have to put the individual ahead of their actions.

I've learned that we don't have to change friends if we understand that friends change.

I've learned that if you don't want to forget something, stick it in your underwear drawer.

I've learned that you shouldn't be so eager to find out a secret. It could change your life forever.

I've learned that the clothes I like best are the ones with the most holes in them.

I've learned that two people can look at the exact same thing and see something totally different.

I've learned that no matter how you try to protect your children, they will eventually get hurt and you will hurt in the process.

I've learned that there are many ways of falling and staying in love.

I've learned that no matter the consequences, those who are honest with themselves, get farther in life.

I've learned that many things can be powered by the mind, the trick is self-control.

I've learned that no matter how many friends you have, if you are their pillar, you will feel lonely and lost at the times you need them most.

I've learned that your life can be changed in a matter of hours by people who don't even know you.

I've learned that even when you think you have no more to give, when a friend cries out to you, you will find the strength to help.

I've learned that writing, as well as talking, can ease emotional pains.

I've learned that the paradigm we live in is not all that is offered to us.

I've learned that credentials on the wall do not make you a decent human being.

I've learned that the people you care most about in life are taken from you too soon.

I've learned that although the word "love" can have many different meaning, it loses value when overly used.

I've learned that it's hard to determine where to draw the line between being nice and not hurting people's feelings and standing up for what you believe.

—Author Unknown

"The wisest mind has something yet to learn."
—George Santayana

Cowboy Mouths

The New Orleans band Cowboy Mouth, which is a fairly tough and aggressive rock band often orchestrates random hugs among tens of thousands of sweaty strangers. It's amazing how Fred can get everyone to the point where it makes no difference if that hug is with a sweaty beer belly or a spokes model (well, maybe some difference) and the compliance level is always high.

—Erik Filkorn

"Whatever you are be a good one."
—*Abraham Lincoln*

Those beside You

During my third year of education, our professor gave us a pop quiz. I was a conscientious student and had breezed through the questions, until I read the last one: 'What is the first name of the woman who cleans the school?" Surely this was some kind of joke. I had seen the cleaning woman several times. She was tall, dark-haired and in her 50s, but how would I know her name? I handed in my paper, leaving the last question blank. Before class ended, one student asked if the last question would count toward our quiz grade. Absolutely, said the professor. "In your careers you will meet many people. All are significant. They deserve your attention and care, even if all you do is smile and say hello". I've never forgotten that lesson. I also learned her name was Dorothy.

"Never look down on anybody unless you're helping them up."
—The Reverend Jesse Jackson

Wearing your "Stuff"
on your Sleeve

We all give off vibes whether we know it or not. I've always been aware of this, and in fact often discuss it when I'm wearing my Love Coach hat and lecturing to singles regarding the need to be conscious of how you come across to the opposite sex.

But it's not just about dating and socializing. It's about how we live our daily lives and how we come across to others. The energy we project and the energy we invite into our lives. This particularly came to my attention during a recent trip.

I was visiting a friend in South Carolina, and we were shopping and browsing in one particular store. She was trying on some skirts and tops, and I was sharing with her where I'm at with my career. I was questioning where I'm heading, discussing the need to attract more monetary opportunities. Talking about some pursuits I've long had on my To Do List, wondering when and if I might get to them one day.

She was listening thoughtfully and lending me a very supportive ear. Out of the blue, the sales girl in the store came over to me, and asked if she could ask me an "odd" question. She didn't want to make me uncomfortable, but wanted to know if it was okay if she gave me a hug. I was pretty taken aback at the moment, but said "sure".

She said she just felt like I needed one. I found that quite curious since she hadn't been listening to my discussion with my friend, and for the moment, I didn't get why she'd think I had that need. But, then it occurred to me that I was feeling a little sad and lost when chatting with my friend, and clearly the universe picked up that vibe. And the sales girl readily tuned into it and reaches out.

How totally sweet that was of her. It was so very touching. And it heightened my awareness of the "stuff" that vibes are made of. Amazing how a tone of voice, body language, energy, etc. when put out there can be so easily picked up by someone with a deep sense of awareness. How supportive for someone to connect with me on that level. It was truly appreciated.

So don't hesitate to wear your "stuff" on your sleeve, because you never know when someone might give you a hug. And the same can be said of you. The more self-aware we become, the better able we are to be there for someone else in need. If we're all caught up with our own stuff, we can't really hear or feel for others. So let it out as best you can. Find an empathetic ear or meditate. But release and invite the positive vibes to take over.

—Robin Gorman Newman

"The miseries of men come from not being able to sit alone in a quiet place."
—*Pascal*

DO IT ANYWAY

People are often unreasonable, illogical, and self-centered;
Forgive them anyway.

If you are kind, people may accuse you of selfish, ulterior motives;
Be kind anyway.

If you are successful, you will win some false friends and true enemies;
Succeed anyway.

If you are honest and frank, people may cheat you;
Be honest and frank anyway.

What you spend years building, someone could destroy overnight;
Build anyway.

If you find serenity and happiness, they may be jealous;
Be happy anyway.

The good you do today, people will often forget tomorrow;
Do good anyway.

Give the world the best you have, and it may never be enough;
Give the world the best you've got anyway.

You see in the final analysis, it is between you and God;
It was never between you and them anyway.

—Mother Teresa

"Light is the task where many share the toil."

—Homer

Life's Major League Curveballs

What do Steve Jobs and Steve Wozniak have in common? Did you answer? Take a moment and come up with an answer. They both co-founded Apple Computers. They both accomplished this feat in a garage, and they both did this in their early 20's. Is that not amazing? What's even more amazing is that within a decade, they turned their garage project into a billion dollar company. Wow!

It seemed that everything was going tremendously well for Steve Jobs, than the unexpected happened. He got fired from the same company he helped create. Imagine that. What would you have done? Instead of quitting, Steve Jobs decided to start all over again. He shook up his innovative spirit and started another company called Pixar, the most successful animation studio in the world.

We all get hit with life's Major League curveballs. As in Steve Job's case, maybe it's getting fired. It could also be the loss of a loved one, a serious illness, an accident or some financial loss. What ever curveball life throws at you, it's up to you to pull yourself back up and turn those negative circumstances into a positive experience. It's not your position in life that matters, but choosing to do what matters most in life that counts.

Who knows, you may become the next Steve Jobs of your life's vocation.

"If your ship doesn't come in, swim out to it."
—*Jonathon Winters*

- Steve Jobs passed away to pancreatic cancer during the writing of this book. God bless him and his family.

Bucket List to Freedom

Do you ever feel burned out, fed up or just plain bored by the monotony day-to-day activities of your life? Ever feel your days are simply passing you by without any noticeable meaning? If so, you are not alone. In fact, at times I've contemplated over these same questions in my mind as well.

If you haven't read the book, *"The Magic of Thinking Big"* by David Schwartz, please do yourself a huge favor, find it and read it. Schwartz writes that anyone who is bored with their current life has simply forgotten how to dream.

David Schwartz invites you to sit down, let your imaginations go wild, write down your own bucket list and dream! According to The Oxford Dictionary, to dream is to: daydream or fantasy, an ambition, a state of mind out of touch with reality.

What items are on your list is entirely up to you. Go on an African safari, learn to speak a new language, or hunt a beluga whale in Canada's north. One thing for certain is that your boredom will have disappeared and you will be living life at a different level. In the words of William Ross, "Every man dies, not every man really lives." Have you written your buck list lately?

"Things that matter most must never be at the mercy of things that matter least."

—Goethe

An Unforgettable Gift

My hug story concerns a 90 year old lady in a senior citizens home over the Christmas holiday. Santa shows up for his rounds after wishing everyone a Merry Christmas and begins chatting with the group. One older woman asks Santa to follow her to her room. Not knowing what she may ask or do, he reluctantly follows.

Once in her room, she asks Santa if he could help an old lady out, to which he replies ok. She then says, "My husband has been dead for many years now, do you think I could have a hug from a nice man like yourself?" Of course Santa was happy to give her a nice hug for Christmas.

She thanked him then sat quietly in her rocking chair, smiling with a tear in her eye, as happy memories went through her aging, but sharp mind of her husband's hugs that once were so long ago.

Alicia M. Strang
Nova Scotia, Canada

"Live your life in the manner that you would like your kids to live theirs.
—Michael Levine

Always Remain Curious

It has been said that Walt Disney never gave in-depth instructions to his staff about what he wanted them to do. Instead, he would point them in the right direction, than the rest was up to them.

In 1923, twenty-one year Walt Disney moved from Kansas to Los Angeles to work in the movie business, but no one would hire him. So Walt hired himself. He rented a camera, set up a studio in his uncle's garage and began making animated cartoons.

In 1934, Walt took a pioneering step and began creating full-length animated feature films, such as Snow White. In 1950, he entered television with the Mickey Mouse Club. And in 1962, he launched a new theme park business, the magical world of Disneyland.

Walt Disney would often say to his artists, "We keep moving forward, opening new doors, and doing new things, because we're curious and curiosity leads us down new paths." What an inspirational leader.

Walt Disney, along with his staff, received more than 950 honors from every nation in the world, including 48 Academy Awards and 7 Emmys. Through his imagination and optimism, Walt Disney touched the hearts and minds of millions worldwide, and that magic continues today. Thank you Walt Disney!

"More gold has been mined from the thoughts of men than has been taken from the earth."

—Napoleon Hill

The Starfish

A small boy lived by the ocean. He loved all the creatures of the sea, especially the starfish, and he spent much of his time exploring the seashores. One day he learned that there would be a minus tide that would leave the starfish stranded on the sand. The day of the tide he went down to the beach and began picking up the stranded starfish and started tossing them back in the sea.

An elderly man who lived next door came down to the beach to see what he was doing. "I'm saving the starfish." The boy proudly declared. When the neighbor saw all of the stranded starfish he shook his head and said, "I'm sorry to disappoint you young man, but if you look down the beach one way, there are stranded starfish as far as the eye can see. And if you look the other way, it's the same. One boy like you isn't going to make much of a difference."

The boy thought about this for a moment. Then he reached down to the sand, picked up a starfish, tossed it back into the ocean and said, "I sure made a difference for that one"

"Too many people go through life waiting for things to happen instead of making them happen."

—Sasha Azevedo

The Wizardly Power of Belief

After she separated from her husband, was diagnosed with clinical depression and struggling with unemployment, J.K. Rowling completed her first novel, "*Harry Potter*" in cafes and restaurants.

In her biography, J.K. Rowling attributed her success to an elementary friend who believed in her as a writer. Talk about the power of belief. Sit back William Shakespeare, because her books have sold nearly 400 million copies and she is the highest earning novelist in history. Because of her incredible success on the New York Times bestseller list, they introduced a bestseller list for children's books. What a tremendous honor to Ms. J.K. Rowling. Never underestimate the power of belief!

Get out there and offer your encouragement to someone today. It may be exactly what they need to accomplish their goals or dreams. Encouragement and compliments are free, but you truly are offering them more than any amount of money could ever buy.

"Life is 10 percent what you make it and 90 percent how you take it."
—*Irving Berlin*

A Picture is worth a Thousand Words

I was out with my camera in the state of Kentucky. My passion is to walk around on my own and hope and pray that I would run into my favorite kind of subjects to photograph. I did on this particular day. I tried to remain far enough way not to interrupt their privacy, but close enough to get a great angle shot.

My subjects were two elderly people in what looks like their eighties. Although she was slowly moving forward with the aid of her husband, she moved so gracefully. I noticed as they approached the bench, that he had his fragile arm wrapped about her tiny waist. It did not appear as if he was trying to aid her, but looked as if his arm was supposed to be right where it was resting, in the small of her back.

I was so touched by what was unfolding in front of me that I continued to stare without the aid of my camera lens. The gentleman gently tugged on her and she looked up at him with a gentle smile as she wrapped her arms around him and very naturally strokes her fingers through his thinning hair. He pulls her close and leans in to sweetly peck her lips and then tucks his head into her hair to welcome the hug.

Ever so briefly I witnessed the love actually pass between this elderly couple. I was so wrapped up in their hug that I forgot to get the actual footage shot. I guess I missed documenting such a wonderful, loving hug, but that memory will remain in my mind forever.

Tamara Bell
PEI, Canada

"Never regret. If it's good, it's wonderful. If it's bad, it's experience."

—*Victoria Holt*

Surfing to Higher Heights

I vividly remember one plane flight in which I watched a movie called, "*Soul Surfer*". The movie was based on a surfer named Bethany Hamilton who lost her left arm to a tiger shark attack while surfing near her home in Hawaii. Three weeks later, Hamilton was back on her board and ready to compete.

Amazingly, Hamilton went on to win numerous national surfing championships. In 2004, she won the Best Comeback Athlete ESPY Award, and was also presented with a special "Courage Award" at the 2004 Teen Choice Awards. In 2005, she took 1st place in the National Scholastic Surfing Association (NSSA) National Championships, and in 2008, she began competing full-time on the Association of Surfing Professionals (ASP) World Qualifying Series (WQS). Bethany Hamilton is truly an amazing person and competitor.

It's easy to be strong when things are going well, but when times get tough, that's when you find out what you're really made of. Her ability to overcome this serious and debilitating injury to ultimately return to professional surfing is a perfect example of how one can change their world. Few people can change the world, but we all have the inner strength to change our world.

"Success is measured by oneself."

—*Helga Sandburg*

Changing the World One Hamburger at a Time

Ray Kroc, the founder of McDonald's is a great example of leaving one's personal signature. Although many did not believe in his fast food concept and the desire to eat out, Ray believed in himself and that's all that mattered.

He standardized operations, ensuring every hamburger would taste the same in Toronto as in Tokyo. He set strict rules on how the food was to be made, cooking methods and times, portion sizes and packaging. Ray Kroc took the risk and built the company into the most successful fast food operation in the world.

"If you have time to lean, you have time to clean," Ray would often say to any idle employee. What's so amazing about his story is that Ray accomplished this idea at the age of 52.

Today, McDonald's restaurants are found in 119 countries around the world, and serve more than 64 million customers a day. That's over 64 million personal signatures a day. Now that's changing the world one hamburger at a time.

"If you only do what you know you can do—you never do very much."
—*Tom Krause*

Wings of Protection

An article in National Geographic several years ago provided a powerful picture. After a forest fire in Yellowstone National Park, forest rangers began their hike up a mountain to assess the damage.

One ranger found a bird literally petrified in ashes, perched on the ground at the base of a tree. Somewhat sickened by the unnatural sight, he knocked over the bird with a stick. When he struck it, three tiny chicks dashed from under their mother's wings. The loving mother, aware of looming danger, had carried her offspring to the base of the tree and gathered them under her wings.

She could have flown to safety, but had refused to abandon her babies. When the blaze had arrived and the heat charred her small body, the mother remained dedicated. Because she had been willing to die, her chicks under the cover of her wings continued to live.

"Courage is not the absence of fear, but rather the judgment that something else is more important than fear."

—*Ambrose Redmoon*

From Punching Bag to World Champion

Most of us have heard of the movie *"Cinderella Man"*, starring Russell Crowe. It was a great movie, but the true story of the hard-nosed, light heavyweight, Irish-American boxer Jim Braddock is far more remarkable.

Jim Braddock was a light heavyweight boxer in the 1920's, in which the sport provided his family with a good living. This drastically changed when the Great Depression hit America and Jim crushed his knockout right hand while working on the docks. The future did not look bright for Jim Braddock.

Many would have felt this was a sure sign that their boxing career was over, that it was time to permanently hang up the gloves. Not Jim Braddock. Although he was merely considered a punching bag for other up-coming boxers, he went on to knock out heavyweight contenders John Griffin, Art Lasky and the ever dangerous Max Baer to become the heavyweight champion of the world.

When his underdog story hit the media, he was labeled "The Cinderella Man," and soon represented the hopes of the American public struggling through the Great Depression. "It's not what happens to you, but how you react to it that matters", said Epictetus so many years ago. In other words, if you don't stand for something, you'll fall for anything.

We do not live in an easy world, nor do we live in an impossible world. Jim Braddock whole heartedly believed in that message. Do you?

> "Tough times never last, but tough people do."
> —Dr. Robert Schuller

A Wife's Never Ending Love

It was almost midnight, Easter Monday, April 25, 2011. Half-dead, I'm lying in the snow at Williamson Lake, Nunavut, Canada. The temperature was—31 degrees celsius with the wind chill. The circumstances of that night immediately changed my best of times into my worst of times.

My whole world collapsed when I read the charges laid against me the next day. I was charged with drinking/driving. The impact was extremely difficult on my personal life and my families. I fell to my knees, grabbed my head tightly with my two hands, and screamed full of regret. It felt like the end of paradise, the end of my life.

Every morning I would awake to battle the pressures, tensions, stress, guilt and the agony of hopelessness. I prayed everyday with God to please help me through this turmoil. It seemed hopeless, but through it all, my wonderful wife remained by my side and gave my hugs and kisses as confirmation of her support. She's such an amazing woman. Her hugs were contagious, transforming my remaining general well being (GWB) into hope and enthusiasm.

Now many months later, my memories of her daily hugs still give me hope and recharge my inner being. I now feel stronger than I did before that dreadful night. I believe that God carried me through the snow that evening. He took care of me so that I could remain with my loving family. A miracle did happen. Glory be to God, Jesus Christ my Lord and my Savior.

Ruel Ruelos
Philippines

> *"The future depends on what we do in the present."*
> —*Mahatma Ghandi*

The Trouble Tree

I'm not certain who the author of this next story is, but I'd like to share the story of The Trouble Tree with you. It's a remarkable story reminding us not to burden our family with troubles they can not do anything about.

It's a story about a carpenter who had a very rough first day on the job. First, he had a flat tire on his way to work, than his electric saw broke, and finally his truck wouldn't start at the end of the day. Not a pleasant first day by any means.

Feeling bad for him, his employer drove him home. He noticed that as the carpenter walked to his front door, he stopped next to a small tree, gently touching the branches with his hands. After a few seconds, he waved good bye and entered the house.

The next day I asked him why he touched that tree, to which he responded, "That's my trouble tree. Troubles don't belong in the house with my family, so I just hang them on the tree, than I pick them up the next morning. However, the next morning there are never as many troubles as the night before."

Having too much of what you don't need, it's difficult to see the things you do need. I encourage all of you to find your trouble tree. If you live in an apartment, than maybe it will be a trouble plant or a trouble wreath. The object that you choose as your trouble tree is not important; the fact that you do it will pay off immensely with your loved ones.

"Try and fail, but don't fail to try."
—*Stephen Kaggwa*

Your Inner Butterfly

In 1963, it is said that Edward Lorenz proposed a meteorological hypothesis that stated, "A butterfly could flap its wings and set molecules of air in motion, which would move more molecules of air, eventually capable of starting a hurricane on the other side of the world."

That's quite the statement and not everyone would agree with his hypothesis (aka butterfly effect), but I think we can all agree that every action we take or don't take will have an impact on the direction of our lives and the lives of others. Simply put, everything you do does matter!

What you do every morning when you wake up until you fall asleep at night may influence millions of lives in a random chain of events. Some of those influences you will be made aware, most you will never know.

Knowing that you may influence the lives of not only those closest to you, but possibly millions you have never met, and probably will never meet, what will you do with your day. What will you choose to do with your "butterfly effect"?

"Whether you think you can or think you can't, you're right."
—*Henry Ford*

Is My Attitude Worth Catching?

William Jennings Bryan once said, "Destiny is not a matter of chance, it is a matter of attitude and choice." I firmly believe this. What many people fail to realize, including myself at times, is that your attitude not only affects you, but also the folks around you.

Like a virus, attitudes are highly contagious. Remember that words are permanent, hearts cannot be unbroken, so be careful what you say. Once and awhile, take a step back and honestly ask yourself . . . "is my attitude worth catching?"

> *"Excellence is not a skill. It is an attitude."*
>
> —*Ralph Marston*

Theory of a Thousand Marbles

I once read an article of a 55 year old man who began to realize that his years were passing him by, that he was on borrowed time and that at any point his time could expire. He figured the average person lived to be about 75, which gave him another twenty years. With fifty two weeks in a year that gave him one thousand weekends left to enjoy.

He called this the *Theory of a Thousand Marbles*. He bought one thousand marbles, put them in a clear container, and placed the container in his office. Every Monday, he would take out one marble and throw it away.

He discovered that as he was losing his marbles, (no pun intended) he focused more on the important elements in his life. "The greatest danger in life is in permitting the urgent things to crowd out the important." (Charles E. Hummel) I'm sure you've heard this before, but it deserves repeating. Every day could be your last, so live to the fullest!

> *"Wherever you go, go with all your heart."*
>
> —*Confucius*

No Laughing Matter

I recall a story of a Southwest Airline flight attendant who announced over the PA system; "Today we have a gentleman on board who's celebrating his 99th birthday and this is the first time he has ever flown. She added, "So on your way out, stop by the cockpit and wish him a happy birthday."

Laughter is an emotional trigger that can sweep away negative thoughts. It can positively change your endorphins, your brain chemistry and your immune system. The World Health Organization has labeled stress a worldwide epidemic. Who decides if you will be happy or unhappy? The answer is—you do. So laugh out loud and laugh often. It just may add a few more years to your lifespan.

"Read books, listen to audios, attend seminars; they are decades of wisdom reduced to invaluable hours."

—Mark Victor Hansen

Pulling Together as a Team

Teamwork is the ability to work together toward a common goal or effort. Consider the following story from the play, *"Some Folks Feel the Rain; Others Just Get Wet"* the next time you think about teamwork.

A man was lost while driving through the country. As he tried to reach for his map, he accidentally drove off the road and into a ditch. Though he wasn't injured, his car was stuck deep in the mud. So the man walked to a nearby farm to ask for help.

"Warwick can get you out of that ditch," said the farmer, pointing to an old mule standing in a field. The man looked at the old mule and at the farmer who just stood there repeating, "Yep old Warwick can do the job." The man wasn't so sure, but he figured he had nothing to lose.

The two men and the mule made their way back to the ditch. The farmer hitched the mule to the car. With a snap of the reins, he shouted, "Pull Fred! Pull Jack! Pull Ted! Pull Warwick!" And the mule pulled the car right out of the ditch.

The man was amazed. He thanked the farmer, patted the mule, and asked," Why did you call all of those other names before calling Warwick?" The farmer grinned and said, "Old Warwick is just about blind. As long as he thinks he's part of a team, he will keep pulling."

"The achievements of an organization are the results of the combined effort of each individual."

—*Vince Lombardi*

Food for Thought

I've always enjoyed the story of the boy and his grandfather. A boy was talking with his grandfather. "What do you think about the world situation?" he asked. The grandfather replied, "I feel like wolves are fighting in my heart. One is full of anger and hatred; the other is full of love and forgiveness. "Which one will win?" asked the boy. To which the grandfather replied, "The one I feed." (Author unknown)

In Dr. Norman Vincent Peale's bestselling book "The Power of Positive Thinking", he often states that you become what you think about. If you think of negative thoughts, than you'll get negative results; but if you choose to think about positive thoughts, than you'll get positive results. Which thought will you feed?

"Our food should be our medicine and our medicine should be our food."
—Hippocrates

Turn Up Your Inner Heat

It's been scientifically shown that at 211 degrees, water is HOT, but at 212 degrees, it BOILS. That boiling water may produce enough steam to move an entire train. One simple degree made all the difference. That same principle applies to you. If you pushed yourself just a little further, just a little harder, imagine what you could do, what you could accomplish.

In the words of the great inventor Thomas Edison, "Many of life's failures are men who did not realize how close they were to success when they gave up." There are no real secrets to success. Success requires three simple, but important elements . . . risk, effort and perseverance. So step out of your comfort zone, take risks, fail, get back up, turn up your inner heat and move "your train" in life.

"Always be a first-rate version of yourself, instead of a second-rate version of somebody else."

—*Judy Garland*

The Top Five Percent

What do you believe would happen to 100 people who start out in life even at the age of 25 by the time they all reach 65? Many years ago a survey was done on this exact question and here are the results. By the time they are 65, only one will be rich, four will be financially free, five will still be working and 54 will be broke.

In the words of Earl Nightingale, "We become what we think about." The human mind contains riches far beyond our wildest imagination. It will return anything we allow it to foster. It's been said that most of us are only using ten percent of our brain. Are you going to sit back and let life take you over? Or will you direct your life into a desired direction? It's up to you.

Albert Einstein was a failure in Math during his elementary school years, yet he grew up to do things mathematically that changed the way we look at the world. I challenge you to control your thinking, control your focus and become the person you want to become.

Become one of the top five percent.

"If you don't make mistakes, you aren't really trying."
—Coleman Hawking

Keep Your Chin Up

Do you watch the Tonight Show? Even if you don't, I'm sure you have heard of their host, Jay Leno. He is widely known for his America-friendly act and his characteristically protruding chin. But Jay wasn't always so fortunate. In his autobiography, he recalls a teacher who made a positive impression on him to go into show business.

Jay and this teacher met in detention hall in the school library, where he unfortunately spent a lot of his time as a student due to his schoolyard pranks and jokes. Jay would consistently make the teacher laugh until one day he said, "You are really funny, why don't you consider going into show business?"

Jay had never thought of that before. That day forward he began seriously thinking about becoming a comedian, making people laugh for a living. He performed everywhere he could. Dirty bars, rowdy clubs, for years he booked over 300 appearances annually. It didn't matter; it was all part of the struggle. Than in 1992 his struggles came to an end. He was offered the opportunity of a lifetime. He was to replace Johnny Carson and become the new host of The Tonight Show.

What are you currently struggling with? Don't give in, keep moving forward and always keep your chin up, because better days are just around the corner. Just ask Jay Leno.

"A real friend is one who walks in when the rest of the world walks out."
—Regina Brett

Living Life through a TV Screen

A recent study by the Nielsen Company, those who record how many people watch TV and how much TV they watch, had this to offer. On average people watch about 6.5 hours of TV each day. In a life span one would spend about eleven years watching TV. That is worth reading again . . . eleven years of your precious life is wasted watching TV.

I suggest you cut back on the amount of TV you watch and start living the life you want to live, the life you deserve to live. Use that extra time to learn a new language, try a new sport, travel to a foreign country, write a book or spend it with your loved ones at home.

I challenge you to turn that TV off right now and do something more meaningful with your life. It's completely up to you what you do with that extra time, but living life through a TV screen should not be one of them.

"The future belongs to those who believe in the beauty of their dreams."
—*Eleanor Roosevelt*

Brotherly Love

Last year my brother died of cancer. I flew home a few months prior to his death so that I could say goodbye. We weren't very close, and I always thought of him as a bully, but strange as it is, I always looked up to him. He was strong and afraid of nothing and I can never remember him saying he loved me or hugging me as a child.

When we met, he was this frail man that seemed a stranger in my brother's clothes. We spent a few days together and on the final day, he walked up to me, told me he loved me and gave me a hug, which turned out to be his last and only hug. I miss him dearly and I will cherish that moment forever.

Denton E. Winn
Vancouver, Canada

"We are made for loving. If we don't love, we will be like plants without water."

—Archbishop Desmond Tutu

Call it Puppy Love

A long time ago, I read a story about a farmer who had some puppies he needed to sell. He painted a sign advertising the four pups, and set about nailing it to a post on the edge of his yard.

As he was driving the last nail into the post, he felt a tug on his overalls. He looked down to see a little boy. "Mister," he said, "I want to buy one of your puppies." "Well," said the farmer, as he rubbed his forehead, "These puppies cost a lot of money."

The boy dropped his head for a moment. Then reaching deep into his pocket he pulled out a handful of change and held it to the farmer. "I've got thirty-nine cents. Is that enough?" "Sure," said the farmer. And with that he let out a whistle. "Here Dolly!"

Out from the doghouse ran Dolly, followed by four little puppies. The little boy pressed his face against the chain link fence. His eyes danced with delight. As the dogs made their way closer, the little boy noticed something else stirring inside the doghouse.

Slowly another little pup appeared, this one noticeably smaller. Down the ramp it slid in an awkward manner. The little pup began hobbling toward the others, doing its best to catch up. "I want that one," the little boy said, pointing to the runt.

The farmer knelt down at the boy's side and said, "You don't want that puppy. He will never be able to play with you like these other dogs." The little boy stepped back, reached down, and began rolling up one leg of his trousers. In doing so, he revealed a steel brace running down both sides of his leg attaching itself to a specially made shoe.

Looking back up at the farmer, he said, "You see sir, I don't run too well either, and he will need someone who understands." With tears in his eyes, the farmer reached down and picked up the little pup. Holding it carefully he handed it to the little boy. "How much?" asked the little boy. "No charge," answered the farmer, "There's no charge for love."

"From every wound there is a scar, and every scar tells a story. A story that says, I survived."

—*Craig Scott*

The Power of Visualization

Canadian Georges St-Pierre (aka GSP) is a mixed martial artist who has dominated his weight class for years and at the time of this writing, is the Welterweight Champion of the UFC. He has often indicated that he uses visualization before his matches.

Saint Pierre would often stand inside the octagon before his fights and visualize his opponent, his training, the match and the announcer raising his hand in victory. This ritual he felt gave him an extra edge over his opponent.

Canadian Olympic gold medalist Mark Tewksbury did the same thing to win the 200 meter backstroke in Barcelona, Spain in 1992. Many other successful people have used the powerful tool of visualization. This is a popular technique for top athletes who know they have to remain in their zone. The zone is where you go when you can do no wrong. You are so connected to your higher self that any fear you have will disappear.

If you copy the techniques of champions, you too can become a champion. Maybe it's to become a better parent, partner, employee or world champion. We must look within ourselves, not once, but again, and again, and again to discover what is most important to us. By investing time and effort into visualizing your dream, you're preprogramming it into your subconscious mind. It's mind over matter. Put yours into action now.

"To get to the top actually, you must get to the top mentally."
—Chris Widener

Don't Quit

When things go wrong as they sometimes will,

When the road you're trudging seems all up hill,

When the funds are low and the debts are high

And you want to smile, but you have to sigh,

When care is pressing you down a bit,

Rest if you must, but don't you quit.

Life is queer with its twists and turns,

As every one of us sometimes learns,

And many a failure turns about

When he might have won had he stuck it out;

Don't give up though the pace seems slow—

You may succeed with another blow,

Success is failure turned inside out—

The silver tint of the clouds of doubt,

And you never can tell how close you are,

It may be near when it seems so far;

So stick to the fight when you're hardest hit—

It's when things seem worst that you must not quit.

By Edgar A. Guest

"You must look into people, as well as at them."
—*Lord Chesterfield*

If you are reading this book over the Christmas holiday, type in the email address below for a Christmas Hug Coupon, and be sure to pass it along to others.

http://click1.todaysnewstuff.com/
xggknggrprqtjvvptpcqrtcjvntgbdhkvbklpjdbjvrgcpvcjfjlqhjj.
html

"Tenderness and kindness are not signs of weakness and despair, but manifestations of strength and resolutions."

—*Kahlil Gibran*

Enough for a Tip

A 10-year-old boy entered a hotel coffee shop and sat at a table. A waitress put a glass of water in front of him. "How much is an ice cream sundae?" "Fifty cents," replied the waitress. The little boy pulled his hand out of his pocket and studied a number of coins in it.

"How much is a dish of plain ice cream?" he inquired. Some people were now waiting for a table and the waitress was a bit impatient. "Thirty-five cents," she said abruptly. The little boy again counted the coins. "I'll have the plain ice cream," he said. The waitress brought the ice cream, put the bill on the table and walked away.

The boy finished the ice cream, paid the cashier and departed. When the waitress came back, she began wiping down the table and then swallowed hard at what she saw. There, placed neatly beside the empty dish, were two nickels and five pennies—her tip.

"Listen with regard when others talk. Give your time and energy to others; let others have their own way; do things for reasons other than furthering your own needs."

—Larry Scherwitz

De-stressing from a Child's Love

I do not really have a story to share, but an everyday thing for me. After all the pressures at work, the traffic, the inevitable stresses of life, at the end of the day when my son hugs me and says "I love you mommy", all the bad things simply up and disappear instantly. It's magic really.

Nika Corales
Bloomington, IN

"If you find it in your heart to care for somebody else, you will have succeeded."

—*Maya Angelou*

I Love You, I Forgive You and Good Night Mother

None of us are immune to the pain and suffering that accompanies tough times. It's through these tough times that we foster strength and character. Within each of us exists the personal power to deal with life's adversities. I woke up that dormant power within myself the day my mother was murdered. I'd like to share with you that story.

June 3rd, 2006, was by far the worst day of my life. I received a shocking, most dreaded phone call. It is the one that every one of us wishes we could avoid, but is inevitable. It came from my younger sister. She reluctantly, yet hysterically informed me that our mother had passed away. Not only had she passed away, but she was brutally stabbed to death in her Toronto apartment. Can it possibly get any worse? Unfortunately, yes it can. She was stabbed to death at the enraged hands of her own son, my stepbrother, who was high on crystal meth. How could this awful tragedy have happened? Please allow me to try and explain.

My mother was born into a family of a very loving, caring Irish mother and a very violent, alcoholic father from Nova Scotia. Being the independent, out spoken daughter that she was, she often heard and felt the wrath of his physical violence. Even worse, she experienced many of his unwanted, sexual advances; such as sneaking into her bedroom at night. As a coping technique, she turned to the bottle, drinking anything she could get her hands on, as her means of escape and continuing the cycle of her father, becoming an alcoholic herself. Her mother and her sisters tried to intervene, but fearing for their own safety and well-being that he might beat them instead, my mother was basically on her own.

She would later go on to marry a Navy man, my father, who was often away at sea more than he was home with his family. Back in the early 1970's, NATO operations took my father away for ten months at a time. My mother had four children of her own, three boys and one girl. She then went through a bitter divorce, losing her children first to Social Services, then to her ex-husband. I feel that she honestly felt that we were better off without her. Now a parent myself, I also believe that she did the best that she could with what she knew and had at that point in her life, but it wasn't enough. At the innocent ages of three to five years old, we often went to bed or woke up hungry, did not attend school, witnessed complete strangers partying in our house and lived a chaotic, unstable life.

At times my mother received welfare when she wasn't working for minimum wage. She depended heavily on the bottle to help her make it through the day and to deal with life's hardships. And we had many of them, as we lived in some of the worst neighborhoods in the city. There were increasing family problems such as constant arguments and violent fights, while all of us kids did our best to stay out of her way due to her constant drinking. In her eyes, the world was a very cruel, unstable place and she found her solace in alcohol, which eventually became her only form of stability. For quite a long time she became another one of society's many functional alcoholics able to hold her job, temporarily tend to her kids, and fool her family and friends into believing that she had it together.

As a result of her constant lies and alcoholic lifestyle, our lives got worse. It was a life in which she placed booze as a priority over her own children. She never really slept at night, but passed out. She didn't always come home and one time we all sat waiting with tears in our eyes, one Christmas morning, for her to come home or at least call us. I recall Truant Officers regularly showed up at our door because we were not attending school. It was horrible. I was the youngest son and while living with my dad, decided at the early age of eleven to cut off all ties with her. I didn't visit, write or call her for any reason. I thought it would make my life easier by staying away from her and the alcoholic lifestyle she chose. So for nearly twenty five years I did just that and knew very little about my own mother. Even though I thought it was a necessity for my own survival, it hurt me that she wasn't in my life. I never shared any of my emotions with anyone.

Through the years I got bits and pieces of information about her from other family members. At one point I heard that she remarried a man and had two more sons. I purposely choose not to get to know either of them. If she wanted to pretend to be a good mother to them, I didn't want to witness it a second time. I also heard both her and the new husband drank heavily, often abusing each other both verbally and physically. I also heard that one of my step brothers was a serious drug user of crystal meth, but I was determined to stay out of her life. Looking back from this day, I wish I had of called her. I wish I had of dropped by to see if she needed anything. I wish I had of told her meth addicted son to move onwards and to leave her the hell alone. More than anything, I wish I could take back June 3, 2006.

For those of you unaware of the dangers of crystal meth, allow me to briefly explain. Crystal meth is methamphetamine hydrochloride. The street form of the drug methamphetamine comes in clear, chunky crystals and is heated and smoked. Other familiar street names are "ice", "glass", and "crystal". With higher doses of methamphetamine, especially if smoked or injected, the user immediately experiences and intense rush, which causes extreme pleasure, lasting only a few minutes. The user quickly becomes dependent and addicted, needing more and higher doses of the drug as the addiction progresses. Thus the downhill, life threatening journey begins.

My step brother was traveling down the same trail as a lot of drug addicts, as I was told that he would often visit his family and friends only looking for some extra money in order to get more of the drugs that supported his habit. In the beginning of his search for money, my mother would reluctantly give it to him. But as time went by, she realized what he was using it for and stopped handing it out. He still kept showing up, giving her sob stories such as he needed money to buy food, purchase a bus pass, pay rent, etc. After listening to his many lies, dealing with his violent outbursts and frequent harassments, my mother got a restraining order against him to leave her alone.

Everything seemed to be going fine for a few weeks until that fatal evening, June 3, 2006, when he once again showed up at her apartment. At first she refused to let him in, but he broke down crying, saying how sorry he was and just wanted to talk to her. She reluctantly let him in. They spoke civilly for a few minutes, but then things started to escalate and quickly got out of control. The bottom line was not a mystery. He was looking for money again. He needed a fix and had nowhere else to turn. When my mom refused to cooperate, his mood quickly changed. According to local neighbors, harsh words were exchanged between them as the argument grew more intense and loud. They saw her cowardly husband leave the apartment for a local bar, leaving her alone to defend herself against a madman high on crystal meth. The outcome was horrific and fatal. He stabbed her with a kitchen knife in the chest and in the neck, than quickly fled the scene, leaving her struggling alone for her life.

A neighbor called 911 and the Police showed up at my mother's apartment at around 8pm only to find her covered in blood. She had been stabbed to death. There was a trail of her blood leading to the telephone nearby, so it was believed that she tried to call for help, but bled to death before she could reach for it. Tipped off by a neighbor who assumed his whereabouts, her son was later found nearby and arrested for murder. My mother's life tragically came to an end at the early age of fifty-nine. It really pains me to think that she tried to get away from violence all of her life, to be at peace and rest comfortably, and ironically she now rests in peace, alone.

I believe what we think about and who we surround ourselves with becomes our reality through our own choices. Having said that, I believe that my mother chose to drink and she chose to live in dangerous circumstances. She chose late nights at the clubs over her children. She chose to stay in bed due to a hangover instead of feeding her children a healthy breakfast and seeing them off to school. She chose many irresponsible, selfish acts, but she did not choose to die and she certainly did not deserve to be murdered. Nobody does.

If life has ever hit you with any type of disturbing events, chances are you will never be the same again. You either cope or you crumple, you become bitter or better, you come out of it stronger or weaker. For me, I choose to take all of my anger and resentment that has grown within me and turn it into something positive. Not only for myself, and for my family, but for anyone else going through or has gone through such a horrific tragedy. I decided to write about this experience in order to help forgive the past and bring some awareness to others concerning the dangers of alcohol and drug addiction and how it tears families apart. It not only influenced my family, but millions of other families at a lesser or greater degree.

I admit that my life has not always been easy, but I feel nothing worthy in life ever is. I do offer advice to those reading this . . . don't feel alone in your current circumstances, seek the help you need. Regardless of where you are in your life right now, know that there are others out there who are going through something similar and you can be as strong as they are and survive the turmoil. You can move forward and change. Decide to change, believe that there has to be change and you can make it happen. You have the information, the willpower and the determination. The only one stopping you is yourself. Just give yourself the confidence and reach out.

In closing, I would like to offer a few words from the great Martin Luther King Jr. He once said, "The ultimate measure of a man or a woman is not where he stands in moments of comfort and convenience, but where he stands in times of challenge and controversy". His words speak of my mother and others like her. Maybe if we gave each other more hugs there would be fewer kids on drugs and less violence in our communities.

As for me, after more than twenty five years of silence and inner reflection, I have a message for her that I hope she can hear from the Heavens above. "I love you, I forgive you, and good night Mother".

Mike Pickles
Nunavut, Canada

"Put all excuses aside and remember this: YOU are capable."
—*Zig Ziglar*

Rocks and Sand

A philosophy professor stood before his class and had some items in front of him. When class began, he picked up a large empty mayonnaise jar and proceeded to fill it with rocks about 2 inches in diameter.

He then asked the students if the jar was full. They agreed that it was. So the professor then picked up a box of pebbles and poured them into the jar. He shook the jar lightly. The pebbles, of course, rolled into the open areas between the rocks.

He then asked the students again if the jar was full. The students laughed and they all agreed it was. The professor picked up a box of sand and poured it into the jar. Of course, the sand filled up everything else.

"Now," said the professor, "I want you to recognize that this is your life. The rocks are the important things—your family, your partner, your health, and your children—anything that is so important to you that if it were lost, you would be nearly destroyed." The pebbles are the other things that matter like your job, your house, your car. "The sand is everything else, the small stuff.

"If you put the sand into the jar first, there is no room for the pebbles or the rocks. The same goes for your life. If you spend all your energy and time on the small stuff, you will never have room for the things that are important to you.

"Pay attention to the things that are critical to your happiness. Play with your children. Take time to get medical checkups. Take your partner out dancing. There will always be time to go to work, clean the house, give a dinner party and fix the disposal. "Take care of the rocks first—the things that really matter. The rest is just sand."

"Once the game is over, the king and the pawn go back in the same box."
—Anonymous

Bad Company

Multibillionaire and business mogul Warren Buffet is one of the best known and most successful investors in the world. It has been noted that one of his business secrets is that he spends a sizeable amount of time meeting with people he may go into business with. If he doesn't like or trust his company, he won't go into business with them. They are considered bad company.

Think about it for a minute. What do successful people want more than anything else? They want to be part of a winning team. They want to contribute to noticeable, tangible results. It's about getting the wrong people off your team and the right people on your team.

Today Warren Buffet and Microsoft founder Bill Gates are best friends. That is one incredible friendship and great company to be with. Together, they are worth billions, but their minds are worth even more.

If you want to be successful, you too must mingle with successful people. There are lots of excellent people out there, spend some time to get to know them and pay attention to your intuition. Take some advice from the 1970's rock band Bad Company and avoid "bad company".

"When you have kept up with the Joneses, there are always the Smiths and the Browns still ahead."

—*Channing Pollock*

Money Matters

I would be remiss if I didn't mention something about money. When it comes to money, time is of outmost importance. To help you reach your financial target sooner than later, I highly encourage you to read the following financial literary gems.

1. *The Millionaire Next Door* by Thomas J. Stanley and William D. Danka
2. *Financial Freedom Without Sacrifice* by Talbot Stevens
3. *Think and Grow Rich* by Napolean Hill
4. *Rich Dad, Poor Dad* by Robert Kiyosaki
5. *The Wealthy Barber* by David Chilton

I wish you all financial freedom. However, don't become the billionaire who sacrifices his entire life to become rich and now wanders from room to room turning off the lights to save a few more pennies. Know when to say enough is enough.

"The real measure of your wealth is how much you'd be worth if you lost all your money."

—*Bernard Meltzer*

What Goes Around Comes Around

One day, while trying to make a living for his family, Farmer Fleming heard a cry for help coming from a nearby bog. He dropped his tools and ran to help. There, stuck to his waist in black muck, was a terrified boy, screaming and struggling to free himself.

Fleming saved the man from what could have been a slow and terrifying death.

The next day, a fancy carriage pulled up to the Scotsman's meager surroundings. A stylishly dressed nobleman stepped out and introduced himself as the father of the boy Farmer Fleming had saved. "I want to repay you," said the nobleman. "You saved my son's life." "No, I can't accept payment for what I did," the Scottish farmer replied, waving off the offer.

At that moment, the farmer's own son came to the door of the family hovel. "Is that your son?" the nobleman asked. "Yes," the farmer replied proudly. "I'll make you a deal. Let me take him and give him a good education. If the lad is anything like his father, he'll grow to a man you can be proud of."

And that he did. In time, Farmer Fleming's son graduated from St. Mary's Hospital Medical School in London, and went on to become known throughout the world as the noted Sir Alexander Fleming, the discoverer of Penicillin. Years afterward, the nobleman's son was stricken with pneumonia. What saved him? Penicillin. The name of the nobleman? Lord Randolph Churchill. His son's name? Sir Winston Churchill.

"A person's true wealth is the good he or she does in the world."

—Mohammed

Your Life's Legacy

In 1980, the first annual Terry Fox Run was held in Canada. Since then, it has grown to involve millions of participants in over 60 countries and is now the world's largest one-day fundraiser for cancer research.

Terry Fox was an athlete, humanitarian, and cancer research activist. When Terry was eighteen years old, he was diagnosed with osteosarcoma cancer, a cancer that would later take his leg. However Terry would not give in to his cancer.

Terry committed himself in the fight against cancer. His Marathon of Hope rose over $24 million dollars. Despite the weather and the pain from his artificial leg, Terry ran for 143 days and a total of 3,339 miles.

Fox remains a prominent figure in Canadian history. His determination united the nation and people from all walks of life. Terry had a purpose in life. His was to find a cure for cancer. When you tap into your inner self, you too will find your passion, your legacy, your life's purpose.

> *"Never give up! Never! Never! Never! NEVER!"*
> —*Winston Churchill*

Secret to Living a Long Life

In an interview with broadcast journalist Barbara Walters, 100 year old comedian George Burns was asked his secret to living a long life. He answered, "I do about 15 minutes of daily stretching and I date younger woman." When asked why he doesn't date women his own age, he quickly replied with a grin, "There aren't any."

Living a long life has some genetic factors, but it's also about attitude and choice. Choose to be happy, choose to laugh and maybe you'll be smoking cigars and dating younger women at the ripe old age of 100, just like George Burns.

"You can't have a better tomorrow if you're always thinking about yesterday."

—C.Roth

Footprints

One night a man had a dream. He dreamed he was walking along the beach with the Lord. Across the sky flashed scenes from his life. For each scene, he noticed two sets of footprints in the sand; one belonged to him, and the other to the Lord.

When the last scene of his life flashed before him, he looked back at the footprints in the sand. He noticed that many times along the path of his life there was only one set of foot-prints. He also noticed that it happened at the very lowest and saddest times in his life.

This really bothered him and he questioned the Lord about it. "Lord, you said that once I decided to follow you, you'd walk with me all the way. But I have noticed that during the most troublesome times in my life, there is only one set of footprints. I don't understand why when I needed you most you would leave me."

The Lord replied, "My precious, precious child, I love you and would never leave you. During your times of trial and suffering, when you see only one set of footprints, it was then that I carried you."

"If someone wants to be a part of your life they'll make an effort to be in it so don't bother reserving a space in your heart for someone who doesn't make an effort to stay."

—*Mitsky*

Find Your "Delete All" Button

I'm betting that you have a to-do list taped to your refrigerator or in your wallet or purse. Most of us lead busy lives with ever expanding to-do lists. Constantly trying to go, go, go and to do, do, do more. And it rarely works. Do you have a stop-doing list?

I recently read that a journalist from Fortune magazine once wrote that when he returned to his office after a two week vacation, over 700 emails awaited him on his computer. 700 emails were screaming for his undivided attention. How overwhelming he must have felt.

Instead of going through all those emails, he held his breath and with a sigh of relief, he pressed the "Delete All" button. He was using his stop-doing list. He then went to work on those projects that really mattered, projects that really demanded his full attention.

Remember the next time that you leave your work place that the world will continue to move without your continuous contact with it. Stop texting or close your email browser and actually take the time to visit a friend or family member. Technology should help you, not hinder you. Become disciplined to unplug your junk.

"Don't worry about the world coming to an end today. It's already tomorrow in Australia."

—*Charles Schulz*

An Honorable 67 Minutes

For almost twenty-seven years, Nelson Mandela was confined to prison due to his thoughts about apartheid. However, he did not give up and later became the next South African President and was the first South African president to be elected in a fully representative democratic election. When you need a dose of motivation, read his inaugural speech.

"Our deepest fear is not that we are inadequate. Our deepest fear is that we are powerful beyond measure. It is our light, not our darkness that frightens us. We ask ourselves, who am I to be brilliant, gorgeous, talented and fabulous? Actually, who are we not to be? You are a child of God. Your playing small doesn't serve the world. There's nothing enlightened about shrinking so that other people won't feel insecure around you. We were born to make manifest the glory of God that is within us. It's not just in some of us, it's in everyone. And as we let our own light shine, we unconsciously give other people permission to do the same. As we are liberated from our own fears, our presence automatically liberates them."

Mandela Day is celebrated on his birthday, July 18, which is an annual international day adopted by the United Nations. Individuals, communities and organizations alike are asked to give 67 minutes to doing something for others, honoring the 67 years that Nelson Mandela gave to the struggle for social justice.

"How far you go in life depends on you being tender with the young, compassionate with the aged, sympathetic with the striving and tolerant of the weak and the strong. Because someday in life you will have been all of these."

—George Washington Carver

Changing the World
One Pencil at a Time

In the summer of 2000, I willingly departed the comforts of Nova Scotia, Canada in exchange for an eye-opening, life changing opportunity to participate in an educational development project in Guyana, South America, on behalf of the Canadian Teacher's Federation. The assignment was called "*Project Overseas.*"

The name Guyana is an Amerindian word meaning "*Land Of Many Waters.*" It is the only country in South America with English as its official language. Not surprisingly, it is famous for its Kaieteur Falls, measuring five times as high as Niagara Falls. I highly suggest you pay Guyana a visit . . . it's a beautiful country.

Our six week assignment was to help improve the teaching methods of Guyanese teachers. Specifically, we were responsible to help them prepare for their up-coming teacher certification examination. Passing this exam meant a pay increase, and since so many lived in poverty, passing was a major priority.

As I sit here and reminisce about my incredible learning experience in Guyana, I find it hard to believe it was so many years ago. I can still vividly recall the day I was eating lunch with the other Canadian teachers, when a convoy of large, military looking trucks pulled into the schoolyard. We all stopped eating and rushed to witness what was happening.

Once parked, the drivers rushed to the back and pulled up the worn, dust-covered tarps. We could not believe our eyes. Hundreds of people exited from the backs of each of those trucks. "Who are these tired, sick looking people?" I asked. Our Supervisor pointed out that they were the Guyanese teachers. They were the teachers who had traveled hundreds, even thousands of miles to be our students.

I was amazed and impressed with the tireless dedication of these teachers towards life-long learning. Many of them made the long journey with their entire families, had not eaten in days, were cramped beyond endurance, and endured the journey through physical illness. They truly understood and appreciated the value of an education. Now **that's** dedication.

Soon all the teachers were unpacked, showered, fed, settled into their quarters and ready to begin classes. The first two weeks were full of lectures, notes, and assignments, which I had planned in advance in the comfort of my own home. I really felt as though I was making a world of a difference in the lives of these less fortunate, less educated Guyanese teachers. Then suddenly all that changed.

One rainy afternoon, I was slowly packing up my teaching supplies when I was distracted by the voice of a woman. As I turned around to identify the soft spoken voice, I saw the face of an older woman. In fact, I was certain she was young in age, but she looked much older. Maybe it was due to life's burdens and hardships, I wondered. She politely approached me, her eyes staring at the floor as if she was ashamed. I stood there silently and waited as she walked towards me. Finally, she stopped in front of me and asked one simple question, a question which would forever change my core beliefs.

"Do you have one spare pencil so that I may break it in half and give it to two of my students?" Not five, not ten, but one pencil is all she asked. Those words brought tears to my eyes. Not having a pencil to offer, and not knowing exactly what to do, I absently searched inside my wallet and gave her a "Hug Someone You Love Today" card. She smiled, looked at the card, gently took it from my hand, hugged me lightly and slowly walked away.

As I watched her leave the classroom, I realized something very important. It struck me how materialistically rich we are in North America, but often spiritually poor. I realized that although we North Americans may have far more money to spend on our educational system, those so called less fortunate teachers had one very important resource to offer their children . . . their love. This and other incidents of kindness and sincerity in Guyana left me convinced that these teachers truly love their students and they truly love to teach. I promised myself that I would take this experience back to my teaching, back to my students. I had to do something. In the words of Helen Keller, "*I am only one, but I am still one. I cannot do everything, but I still can do something. I will not refuse to do the something I can do.*"

There is no doubt in my mind that the Guyanese teachers did learn from us that summer, that we did increase their pedagogical knowledge and improve their teaching skills. Fortunately for me, I learned just as much, if not more from them. I left all my teaching materials there and I proudly returned to Canada with so much more to offer my students . . . more love and hope.

I would like to conclude with a story of the Chinese bamboo tree, which I read in a book from my favorite author and speaker, Zig

Ziglar. The Chinese plant bamboo; they seed, they water and fertilize it, but the first year nothing happens. The second year they water and fertilize it, and nothing happens. The third and fourth years they water and fertilize it, and still nothing happens. The fifth year they water and fertilize it, and sometime during the fifth year, in a period of approximately six weeks, the Chinese bamboo tree grows roughly ninety feet.

"Did the tree grow ninety feet in six weeks or did it grow ninety feet in five years?" Of course it grew ninety feet in five years with the constant nourishment and the unfaltering devotion of the farmer. Now imagine your students as the bamboo seed and you, the teacher, as their water and fertilizer. In your hands, you hold the seeds of failure or the potential for growth. What a huge responsibility, but what a great privilege as well.

Personally, there is nothing else that I would rather be doing with my precious time than offering hope, self-improvement, motivation and re-energizing both myself and others in life.

I hope that reading this chapter was as entertaining and educational for you as it was for me to write. However, this writing was not simply meant to educate or entertain you, but rather to offer you inspiration. Life is meant to be lived. So go out there and challenge yourself. Make mistakes, travel, read, inspire others, and live life to the fullest. Just don't forget to be kind to yourself, your family and friends, and to the environment along the way.

Until our paths cross again, remember what Ralph Waldo Emerson once said, *"What lies behind you and what lies before you are tiny compared to what lies within you."* The next time you feel like giving up, think about the Chinese bamboo tree or think about those dedicated, persistent Guyanese teachers . . . and don't forget to carry a few EXTRA PENCILS!

Mike Pickles
Nunavut, Canada

How Much Is Time Worth?

There was once a little boy who greeted his father as he returned home from work, "Daddy, how much do you make an hour?" Giving his boy a glaring look, the father replied: "Son, don't bother me now, I'm tired." "But Daddy, tell me please! How much do you make an hour," the boy insisted.

Giving in, the father finally replied: "Twenty dollars per hour." "Okay, Daddy could you please loan me ten dollars?" the boy asked. Showing restlessness the father yelled back, "So that was the reason you asked how much I earn? Go to sleep and don't bother me anymore!"

Later that night the father was thinking over what he had said and was feeling guilty. Maybe he thought his son wanted to buy something. Trying to ease his mind, the father went into his son's room.

"Are you asleep?" he asked. "No Daddy. Why?" replied the boy partially asleep. "Here's the money you asked for earlier," the father said. "Thanks Daddy!" rejoiced the son, while putting his hand under his pillow and removing more money. "Now I have twenty dollars!" "Daddy, could I please buy one hour of your time?"

Final Curtain Call

This is my last chapter, but I sincerely hope that my hug stories and my signature stories have offered you some hope and inspiration. In closing, I leave you examples of other remarkable, inspirational people.

- blind/deaf Helen Keller who overcame her disability to teach many others
- the founder of the Missionaries of Charity, Mother Teresa, who never stopped helping the poor until her death in 1997
- actor Michael J. Fox and legendary boxer Mohammed Ali and their daily struggles with Parkinson's Disease
- musician Stevie Wonder who continues to create visual masterpieces through his songs, yet he has been blind since birth
- theoretical physicist and cosmologist Stephen Hawking who continues to do staggering scientific work while crippled with Lou Gehrig's Disease

Nature or what the Chinese call the Tao, has given each of us the gift of life and a distinctive accumulation of talents. You may not be thankful for everything in your life, but you can be thankful for something.

Those people mentioned above are amazing human beings. They became who they are, not from hiding from life's difficulties, but by facing them head on. One thing is for certain; sidestepping our fears won't help. We must face them straight on. These people, like so many others mentioned throughout this book, and so many others unmentioned, faced their fears head on and left their personal signatures to inspire others.

Benjamin Franklin once said, "Some people die at age twenty-five and aren't buried until they're seventy-five." Don't let that person be you. Don't leave this passage on earth with gas left in the tank. Go full out! Demand more from yourself and give it all you've got. You deserve it.

We can all change our life's story by changing what we write today, one word at a time. Or in this case, one hug at a time. If you have a hug story you'd like to share, please write to me at mike_sabbie@ yahoo.ca.

I'd like to leave you with a final message from Mahatma Gandhi, a man who defeated the mighty British Empire using nonviolence. "In a gentle way, you can shake the world." Until we meet again, I challenge you to leave your personal signature and to *change your world one hug at a time.*